Contents

We deliberately haven't put any _essay_ answers in this book, because they'd just be repeating what's in the revision guide. Instead, we've put in a section about how to write good essay answers, and do well. Answers for the _numerical_ questions are included though, on pages 77-78.

How Businesses Work

Here's a bit of background for you. You'd be hard-pushed to get as far as your A-levels and not have some idea about what a business is, but there's a bit more to it than that. Here's the basics on how to start up your own business.

There are **Advantages** to owning a **Business**

1) People set up businesses mainly to make a **profit**. This means a firm **makes** more money than it **spends**. Starting a business is risky, but many people take the risk because of the possibility of big **financial rewards**.

2) People usually only set up their own business if they expect to make **more** than they could earn working as an **employee** of another company.

3) People may set up their own business so that they can be **their own boss** and make their own decisions — they don't have to answer to anyone else.

4) Setting up your own business also gives you the opportunity to do a job you're really **interested** in.

What Ian didn't realise was that if he had his own business, he wouldn't have to answer to anyone.

Most **Businesses** exist to make a **Profit**

1) Businesses aim to make a profit by selling **products** or **services** to customers who are willing to **pay** for them — e.g. a paperclip manufacturer sells a product, and a hair salon sells a service.

2) Some businesses sell **necessities** — products or services that you **need** (like gas and electricity). Other firms provide **luxury** products or services — things you **want** but don't need (like holidays and jewellery).

3) Businesses have to **make a profit** or **break even** (see p.28) to survive.

4) This is especially true in the **private sector** — if a business doesn't make enough money to survive it could go **bankrupt** and have to **close down**.

> Public sector = government-owned
> Private sector = privately owned

5) In the **public sector**, it's not as clear-cut. Organisations like the army, the police, hospitals and state schools aren't there to **make money** — they provide a service to the community. **Charities** are another exception. For more on not-for-profit businesses, see p.17.

Businesses can have **Other Objectives** too

As well as making a profit, businesses may have **other objectives**, such as:

- Offering the **highest quality** goods and services possible.
- Attempting to grow by increasing their **market share**, opening **more outlets** or **taking over** another business.
- Giving good **customer service**.
- Having a good **image** and **reputation**.
- Trying to limit their **impact** on the **environment**.
- **Diversifying** by offering a wider range of products or services.
- **Surviving**. This is essential for **new businesses**, especially in competitive markets (see p.72). It's also important when there's a weak economy (see p.59).

> The size of a company has a big impact on its objectives. An independent shop owner will tend to focus on trying to survive, while a big international company will pay more attention to its corporate image and is likely to try to diversify its product range.

Businesses might **give up some profit** to help them meet **other objectives**. However, most business owners are **ultimately** only interested in **profit**. Everything else comes **after**.

How Businesses Work

Businesses have several different Functions

Production of products or services isn't enough on its own — businesses have **other tasks** to do before they can **make a profit**. These different tasks are usually looked after by different departments.

Business departments and their roles

Production	A business turns **raw materials** into a finished **good** or **service** that they can sell. They must also monitor the **quality** of what they are producing. For more on turning raw materials into goods and services, see p.4. For more on quality, see p. 48-49.
Finance	Businesses have to keep a careful eye on their finances. They must keep detailed and accurate **financial records**. A business must try to get the best **value for money** for every pound it spends. For more on finance, see Section 2.
HRM	**(Human Resources Management)** Businesses must make sure they have the right number of employees of the right quality in the right place at the right time. HRM is on p.40.
Marketing	Businesses have to identify what customers **want** or **need** and figure out how best to **sell** it to them. For more on marketing, see Section 5.
Admin	Businesses have to **run their own affairs** as efficiently as possible.
R&D	**(Research and Development)** Businesses may need to discover **new ideas** for products that might be wanted in the future, and get them ready to be launched onto the market. For more on new product development, see p.60-61.

1) Businesses need to **plan** what activities to do in the future.
2) They need to **control** what workers in the business are doing, and control the amount of money that's spent.
3) Businesses need to **coordinate** all their different functions and departments and make sure that all the departments are working towards common objectives.

Businesses all need certain Key Things

Before businesses can sell things and make a profit, they need certain things:

There's more on different sources of finance on p 18-19.

1)	**Labour**	Businesses need people to do the work.
2)	**Finance**	It costs money to provide goods and services.
3)	**Customers**	Every business needs people to buy the goods and services, and pay for them.
4)	**Suppliers**	Suppliers provide raw materials, equipment and human resources.
5)	**Premises**	Businesses need buildings to work in.
6)	**Enterprise**	Entrepreneurs come up with original ideas and take risks to make a profit.

Practice Questions

Q1 Give three benefits of owning your own business.
Q2 What objectives might a private sector business have? Which objective is the most important and why?
Q3 Give five examples of departments that you might find in a typical business.
Q4 Name at least four essential things that a business needs to produce goods and services.

Exam Questions

Q1 Suggest why Anna White, a fashion designer, might want to leave her job designing clothes for a high street store and set up her own business. (6 marks)

Q2 Discuss the idea that businesses exist to make a profit. (10 marks)

Some businesses only have one function — the office Christmas party...

This first section covers fairly basic business ideas. If you've done GCSE Business Studies, some of it might seem a bit dull. Don't assume you already know it all though — it's worth reading through to make sure you really know what's what. Some of these things will crop up again later in the book — so stick with this section. And then go on to the good stuff...

What Businesses Do

If you're wondering what businesses actually do then you've come to the right page. Businesses are involved in transforming raw materials into finished products, or providing services, and they try to make a profit along the way.

Businesses **Add Value** to raw materials

1) Businesses **pay** for raw materials, then **transform** them into finished products and **sell** them. Customers pay more for the finished product than the business originally paid for the raw materials used to make it.

2) The difference between the **cost** of the raw materials bought by the business to make each product and the **price** the customer pays for the finished product is known as the **value added**.
E.g. if a bakery buys the ingredients for a cake for **80p** and sells the finished cake for **£3**, the value added is £3 − £0.80 = **£2.20**.

3) The value added leaves a **surplus** — the business uses that to pay its other costs (like wages, rent and electricity — see p. 26 for more on costs), and any money left over after this is **profit**.

4) Some products have **high** value added — usually **luxury** items like designer clothes or meals in expensive restaurants. Other products, like basic grocery items, have much **lower** value added.

5) The greater the **value added**, the higher the **profits** are likely to be — businesses want the value added to be as high as possible in order to increase their profits.

Betty had plenty of raw materials — now all she needed to do was work out how to add value.

The **Supply Chain** is the product's journey from **Raw Materials** to **Consumer**

1) **Raw materials** (also called resources or input) go through various stages on their way to reaching the consumer as **finished products** (output). These stages are sometimes called **transformation** and they all form part of the **supply chain**.

2) The supply chain always starts with **raw materials** and finishes with the **consumer**, and the intermediate stages usually include suppliers (businesses that sell products to other businesses), manufacturing, distribution getting products into shops so customers can buy them) and retailers. The supply chain can be short or long depending on the product.

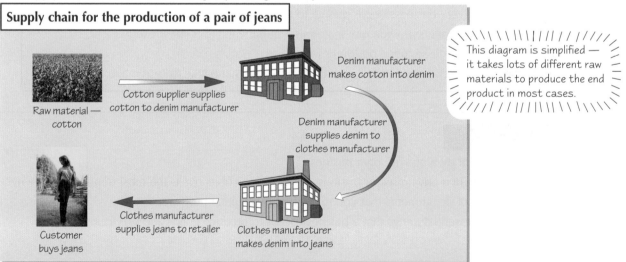

Supply chain for the production of a pair of jeans

Raw material — cotton

Cotton supplier supplies cotton to denim manufacturer

Denim manufacturer makes cotton into denim

Denim manufacturer supplies denim to clothes manufacturer

Clothes manufacturer makes denim into jeans

Clothes manufacturer supplies jeans to retailer

Customer buys jeans

This diagram is simplified — it takes lots of different raw materials to produce the end product in most cases.

3) The various steps in the supply chain often happen in different businesses and different places.

4) All businesses — wherever they are in the supply chain — are dependent on their **suppliers** and **customers** — e.g. a problem with cocoa bean crops in Africa might cause a problem for a shop selling chocolate bars in England.

5) **Value** is normally added at **each stage** in the supply chain — e.g. a bead-making factory turns plastic into beads, which can then be sold for more than the plastic was worth. If a handbag manufacturer uses the beads to decorate handbags, the handbags will be sold for more than it cost the manufacturer to buy the fabric and beads.

What Businesses Do

Businesses can be classified by Production Stage

You can classify businesses according to what **stage** of the **production process** (from raw material to finished product) the business is involved in. There are three divisions — **primary**, **secondary** and **tertiary**.

Primary Sector

1) These are industries that **extract raw materials** from natural resources.

2) This sector covers the **farming**, **fishing** and **mining** industries.

3) Primary sector industries are in **decline** in the UK, mainly because it is often **cheaper** to **import** raw materials from other countries, and trade barriers have made it more **difficult** for UK companies to **export** raw materials. E.g. in 1984 there were **170** coal mines open around the UK — more than **150** of these have now been **closed**.

4) There has also been a decline in the number of people employed in **farming** — the number of people working in farming in the UK is now **less than half** what it was at the start of the 1970s.

Secondary Sector

1) The secondary sector **processes** the raw materials that come from the primary sector.

2) Secondary industry includes **manufacturing** (e.g. cars, tinned food, steel) and **construction** (e.g. building houses, factories, roads).

3) Secondary sector industries have also been **declining** in the UK for the past 25 years, mainly due to companies **moving** production to other parts of the world where manufacturing costs are **lower**. This increases their profits because they can still sell their products to UK consumers at the same price, despite producing them more cheaply. E.g. in 2006, **645** jobs were lost at Nestlé®'s chocolate factory in York when Nestlé® moved production of several products to Europe.

Tertiary Sector

1) This is the **service sector** which provides services (like banking) to **businesses** in the primary and secondary sectors and so helps them to sell their goods, e.g. shops, banks, insurance companies, restaurants, hotels, and healthcare services. It also includes some **direct personal services** to individuals.

2) In most developed countries the tertiary sector has **expanded** over the last few decades — the UK economy is now mainly made up of tertiary sector companies.

3) The main tertiary sector growth in the UK has been in **financial** and **business** services like banking and accounting — the proportion of people working in these jobs in the UK has **doubled** in the last 25 years.

Jon was glad to hear that the tertiary sector was on the increase — he'd always wanted to be an accountant.

Practice Questions

Q1 Give two examples of products with high value added.

Q2 What is the supply chain?

Q3 Give an example of: a) a primary sector business, b) a secondary sector business, c) a tertiary sector business.

Q4 Which is the main production sector in the UK?

Exam Question

Q1 Prawnfree Ltd sell salmon fishcakes. Analyse the effect that a drop in salmon supplies might have on their supply chain.

(10 marks)

I'm in the middle of a (supply) chain reaction...

The whole point of businesses is to add value to whatever they buy so that they can sell it for more than they paid for it — simple really. Learn the definitions of primary, secondary and tertiary sector businesses and a couple of examples of each in case you're asked for them in the exam. And don't forget about the supply chain — it affects all businesses.

Enterprise and Entrepreneurs

Starting a small business is easy, but making a living out of it is blimmin' hard. The examiners want you to show that you understand that starting a successful small firm is not just about having an idea.

People who start businesses are called **Entrepreneurs**

1) An entrepreneur is a person (or one of a group of people) who **raises the resources** and **organises the activities** needed to **start a business**.

2) Entrepreneurs have an **idea** for new businesses, then they organise everything they need to set up their business, including financial investment, staff, buildings, research and development, and marketing.

3) If the entrepreneur **organises** things well, and consumers **want** the good or service, the business will succeed. If they get it **wrong** the business will have to give up and stop trading.

> EXAMPLE: **Richard Branson** was only 20 when he set up **Virgin** as a mail-order music retailer. He then **expanded** the company to include a record shop and recording studio, and he has since continued the expansion successfully — it now includes air travel, mobile, internet, rail and music services. Richard Branson is now one of the **wealthiest** men in Britain, and he was **knighted** for services to business in 1999.

Entrepreneurs are **Innovative Risk-takers**, **Planners** and **Organisers**

1) Successful entrepreneurs tend to be **creative** — they're **innovators** who have spotted a **gap in the market**. A gap in the market is either an **original idea**, or a way of making an **existing** idea **different** from the competition, e.g. selling goods to a new segment of the market.

2) They have **perseverance**. James Dyson took years to get his new design of vacuum cleaner to the market because he couldn't get an existing manufacturer to adopt his ideas. Eventually, he raised the **finance** himself and started his **own small business** to make what's now one of the best-selling cleaners in the world.

3) They're **risk-takers**. When starting a business, many entrepreneurs have to use their **own financial resources** to provide start-up capital. If the business fails, they lose their investment. They're **prepared** to take the risk because they believe that they will gain financial **rewards** — they're motivated by **profit**. As a general rule, low risk = low rewards, and high risk = high rewards.

4) They're good **organisers** and **planners**. Successful entrepreneurs plan what financial, technical and human resources they'll need and organise resources so that they're used cost-effectively.

Entrepreneurs research **Profitable Business Opportunities**

1) Entrepreneurs get ideas for new businesses from **brainstorming** or from personal or professional **experience**.

2) They need to consider the strengths and weaknesses of each idea. E.g. there might be lots of demand for a new Italian restaurant, but no suitable premises to locate the business in.

3) Successful entrepreneurs won't **commit** large resources to an idea until they're confident it will **work**. They need to be sure that there's enough **demand** for their product or service and that they have the **skills** to produce it.

4) Entrepreneurs need to figure out how much money they'll make — it's only worth going ahead with a business idea if it's **profitable**. If they're not likely to make big profits then it's not worth the **risk**.

5) A new business won't usually attract customers unless it can offer something different — a **unique selling point**. This could be quality, low price, good customer service etc.

6) It's really important to get the **price** right. If the price is too high, sales will be too low to make enough money. If the price is too low, the total revenue won't be enough to cover the costs.

The **Government** encourages **Enterprise**

1) The UK government encourages entrepreneurs to set up businesses because enterprise benefits the **economy** — new businesses **increase productivity** and create **new jobs**. The government is especially keen to promote enterprise in areas that need economic **regeneration**.

2) The government has set up organisations like **Business Link** to provide **advice** and **support** to owners of small businesses and to people thinking of starting their own business. They can offer advice on many aspects of setting up and running a small business, including creating a business plan and financing a new business.

3) The government also provides **grants** and **incentives** for entrepreneurs to set up businesses. Entrepreneurs can get grants from various sources, including local authorities and **Regional Development Agencies** like Yorkshire Forward and Advantage West Midlands (see p. 21 for more on this). The **Enterprise Investment Scheme** is another government scheme that offers tax incentives to people who invest in small businesses.

Enterprise and Entrepreneurs

Entrepreneurs have to do **Market Research** on a **Small Budget**

1) Before start-up, it's important to get to know the **market**. Entrepreneurs need to know about the social, environmental, legal and economic factors that limit how they market their product.

2) New businesses can easily do **secondary research** (looking at data that's already available) on a **small budget**, and they can also do low-budget **primary market research** (gathering new data) — this may be a **survey** asking potential customers their opinions of the idea, or **observation** of activities in a similar business.

3) It's really important to be **objective** and **scientific** when doing your own primary research. It's easy and tempting to ask **loaded questions** that lead people into giving the answer you want. It's easy to ask **friends** and **family** who give "nice" answers out of politeness. Watch out for this in exam questions — the new business owner in the case study may have done **unreliable** market research. You'd be spot-on to **question** their methods and their findings. For more on market research, see p. 12-13.

Entrepreneurs have to do **Marketing** on a budget too

1) At the start, a new business doesn't have loads of money to spend on **advertising** campaigns. An advert in the **local paper** and a few cheaply printed **leaflets** are going to be the limit.

2) **Sales promotions** can be **cheap** to organise. Special offers like "buy one, get one free" tend to get people buying.

3) It's important to not stimulate demand **too much** — when demand is greater than the **capacity** of the business, the business has to turn customers away, which isn't good for customer relations, to say the least...
For more on marketing, see p. 11.

New businesses often **Fail**

New start-ups are **risky** — lots of small businesses **fail** within a couple of years of starting up. The reasons for this vary from business to business, but it's often because:

> Nearly all new businesses have limited resources so they have to be very careful about what they spend when setting up.

1) The entrepreneur lacks **experience**. Small business owners, especially **sole traders** (see p.14), have to be a "Jack of all trades" — they're responsible for running all aspects of the business, including finance, managing employees, marketing, etc. Many entrepreneurs don't have enough experience to do all these things properly.

2) Entrepreneurs may have false **expectations** of what running their own business will be like — they expect huge profits or lots of free time, and give up when their expectations aren't met.

3) Many businesses fail because they simply run out of **money** — entrepreneurs sometimes underestimate costs, or overestimate demand or sales, and the business fails because of a **cash flow** crisis (see p.30-31).

4) If a business has an **inaccurate** or **unrealistic** business plan to start with, it's likely to fail.

5) Unexpected delays or a lack of available supplies can cause a business to fail — this is **poor stock control**.

6) Not doing enough **market research**, or not making sure that the research is reliable can also be a cause of failure.

7) The wrong **location** can cause a business to fail, as can changing **market conditions**, such as a recession.

Practice Questions

Q1 Why does the government encourage entrepreneurs to start their own businesses?
Q2 Give three personal characteristics of a successful entrepreneur.
Q3 Why is it important to get the price of a product right?
Q4 Give three reasons why a new business might fail.

Exam Question

Q1 Johan Möller has invented a new tin-opener, and he is setting up his own business to make and sell it.
(a) Discuss where Johan might get help with setting up his business. (4 marks)
(b) Outline two possible strengths and two possible weaknesses of Johan's idea (4 marks)

All you need is an idea... and lots of research... and the right attitude...

Starting a new business sounds like a great idea — you get to be your own boss, and hopefully make loads of money to spend on fast cars and bling. But it can be scary — there are an awful lot of things to be responsible for. It seems that entrepreneurs have to do a heck of a lot of legwork to find out what the market's like and what they need to do to succeed.

New Business Ideas

Before setting up a small business, entrepreneurs need to be sure that they can make money out of their ideas.
If they don't have any business ideas of their own, starting a franchise business instead can be a good option.

Entrepreneurs can target Niche or Mass Markets

Jeffrey and Phil were convinced there would
be a mass market for their origami tableware.

1) Some business ideas are aimed at a **mass market** — they are goods or services that are designed to appeal to **lots of consumers** e.g. Coca-Cola®. Mass markets generally have a **high volume** of sales, but fairly **low profit margins**.

2) Other products may be aimed at a **niche market** — a **smaller** and **more specific** group of consumers. E.g. a new type of fishing bait is unlikely to appeal to people who don't go fishing, but could still generate a good profit if it sold well to fishermen.

3) **Small businesses** can be more successful if they focus on **niche markets** — this often means they don't have to compete **directly** with larger businesses, (who don't normally target niche markets because they can find bigger rewards elsewhere). E.g. if an entrepreneur wants to set up a small business selling microwave meals, they could **establish a niche** by **specialising** in, say, meals for people with nut allergies — this allows the business to make a profit even though there are lots of large ready-meal businesses. Niche markets often have high profit margins, because there's a big **difference** between what it **costs** to make something, and what it can be **sold** for.

4) Small niche **markets** suit small niche **manufacturers**. A small manufacturer can **meet the demand** of a **small segment** of the market. It might not be able to meet the demand of a **mass market**.

Entrepreneurs need to Know the Market

1) Entrepreneurs need a good **background knowledge** of the market they want to sell to — it's much easier to know what will sell well in a particular market if you have **personal experience** of that market. E.g. if you don't know anything about dancing it's probably a bad idea to design a new type of dancing shoe — you won't know what dancers want or need.

2) When they're designing a new product, entrepreneurs need to check if any **similar products** are already on the market — otherwise they could waste time inventing something that's **already** been invented, or coming up with a product that's **less suitable** than what's already available. If there are plenty of competitors in the market already, there might not be any demand for a new product unless it's offering something different.

3) Just because a product hasn't been invented before **doesn't** mean that it'll be commercially successful — some things simply aren't profitable, or won't catch on even if they're original.

Original Ideas are business Assets that can be Protected by law

Businesses and individuals who produce **original work** and earn an income through it need to **protect their ideas** from being copied by others. You can get protection in several ways, depending on what is being protected:

1) A patent is a way of registering and protecting a new invention

If you have a new invention, you can apply for a **patent** from the **Patent Office** (a government agency that checks that an invention is an original design). If you have a patent for your **product**, or your **method** for producing it, no one else can copy it unless you give them a **licence** — and you can **charge** for the licence.

2) Trademarks (™) protect logos and slogans etc.

If you want to protect your business' name, logo or slogan, you can register it as a **trademark** (™) so that nobody else can use it. E.g. the McDonald's golden arches logo is the **intellectual property** of the McDonald's Corporation and it can't be used by any other company. McDonald's promote a certain **brand image** — if the logo was used by other companies, McDonald's **reputation** might be damaged. McDonald's might also lose **profits** if consumers went to another restaurant by mistake because it had the same logo.

3) Copyright gives protection to written work and music

It's **illegal** to reproduce other people's work without their permission. Authors and musicians or their publishers receive **royalties** (payment) every time their work is published or played on the radio.

Franchises

Franchises are *Special Agreements* between *One Business* and *Another*

1) Franchises aren't really a type of business ownership as such. They're **agreements** (contracts) which allow one business to use the **business idea**, **name** and **reputation** of another business.

2) The **franchisor** is the business which is willing to sell, or license, the use of its idea, name and reputation. The **franchisee** is the business which wants to use the name.

3) Several well-known retail chains in the UK operate as franchises, e.g. KFC®, BURGER KING®, McDonald's, Pizza Hut® and The Body Shop®.

The franchisee gets these benefits from running a franchise business:

1) A **well-known name**.

2) A **successful** and **proven** business idea — there is **less risk** of a franchise failing than a totally new business

3) **Training** and **financial support** to set up a new franchise outlet.

4) **Marketing**, **advertising** and **promotion** are done **nationally** by the franchisor.

5) **Buying** is done **centrally** by the franchisor — this helps franchise **outlets** keep **costs** down.

6) Expensive equipment can be **leased** from the franchisor.

7) It can be **easier to finance** a business if it's a franchise — banks can be **more willing** to lend money to people who want to buy a franchise from an established franchisor rather than set up a business from scratch.

A franchise business has these drawbacks for the franchisee:

1) They have to **pay** the franchisor for the right to use the name.

2) They have to pay the franchisor part of the **profits** or an **agreed sum**.

3) They have to run the business according to the franchisor's **rules** — they can't choose their own decor, etc.

4) It might be difficult to **sell** the franchise — they can only sell it to someone the franchisor approves of.

5) The franchise could get a **bad reputation** if other franchisees give bad customer service or sell sub-standard products.

The franchisor gets these benefits from franchising their business:

1) Someone else **runs** bits of their business for them and saves them **wage** costs.

2) They **get paid** for the use of their name, and they get a share of the **profits**.

3) The more franchises there are, the faster the **name** of the business can be **spread**.

4) The **risk** involved in opening an outlet in a new location is **reduced** because the franchisee takes on some of the risk.

A franchise business has these drawbacks for the franchisor:

1) They have to **help** the franchisee set up a new franchise.

2) They provide a good business **concept**, but they have to **share** the rewards with the franchisee.

3) If their franchisees don't have good standards, the franchisor's brand could get a **bad reputation**.

Practice Questions

Q1 What's the difference between a mass market and a niche market?

Q2 How can entrepreneurs legally protect new inventions?

Q3 What's the purpose of copyright?

Q4 What's meant by the terms "franchisee" and "franchisor"?

Exam Question

Q1 Evaluate the advantages and disadvantages of franchising, for both the franchisor and the franchisee.

(10 marks)

I always thought patents were just really shiny leather shoes...

There's lots to learn on these pages, but don't let that get you down — just keep going over all the information until you're sure you've learnt it all. You need to know how entrepreneurs identify and protect a gap in the market, and understand how franchises work — don't forget to learn the advantages and disadvantages for the franchisee and franchisor too.

Understanding Markets

Businesses make a profit if they provide products that customers want or need. In order to do that, they need to understand the market they're trying to sell to, and find out what customers actually want and need.

Markets *are where* Sales Happen *— they aren't* Limited *to a* Physical Place

The market is where the buyer and seller meet. Traditionally the term "**market**" meant the physical **place** where people traded their goods — now it can mean **websites**. "Market" also describes the **type** of **product or service** being bought and sold — e.g. the leisure market, the computer hardware market, the global oil market.

1) **Industrial markets** are where businesses sell to other businesses, such as wholesalers supplying retailers.

2) **Consumer markets** are where firms sell to individual customers — e.g. high street shops like Currys and Next.

3) **Local markets** are where firms sell to customers who live nearby. Selling to a **national market** means selling to people who live all over the country.

4) **Electronic markets** are **virtual markets** where customers don't physically interact with sellers — instead, buying and selling is done over the internet through websites like eBay™ and Amazon.co.uk®. Firms in electronic markets that sell to other companies are called "**business-to-business**" (**B2B**) companies, and the ones that sell to individual customers are called "**business-to-consumer**" (**B2C**) companies.

Market Analysis *tells a* Business *about the* Market *it's in*

Market analysis lets businesses spot **opportunities** in a market by looking at **market conditions**. The most important conditions are **market size**, **growth** in the market and **market share**.

> The more a firm understands about their market, the more likely they are to make good marketing decisions.

MARKET SIZE — by volume and by value

Businesses estimate the size of their market by the **total number of sales** (volume of sales) in the **whole market** or by the **value** in pounds of **all the sales** in the market. Market size is calculated by adding together all the sales made by different firms operating in a particular market. E.g. if there are three firms in the confectionery market, and Firm A sells £526 000 of products, Firm B sells £497 000 of products and Firm C sells £977 000 of products, the market size is £2 million.

> Market size and share have to be considered together. E.g. 10% of a £1m market is worth £100k, while 25% of a £200k market is only worth £50k.

MARKET SHARE — sales as a percentage of total market size

Businesses like to know what **share** of the market they have. If **1 out of every 4** PCs bought was a Dell™, this would mean that Dell™ had a **25% market share** (in terms of units sold). If **£1 out of every £10** spent on perfume was spent on Chanel, this would mean Chanel had a **10% market share** (in terms of sales value).

Market share = sales ÷ total market size × 100%

MARKET GROWTH

Businesses need to know if the market is **growing** or **shrinking**. Competition is fierce in a shrinking market — there are fewer customers to go around. In a **growing** market, **several** firms can **grow easily**. Businesses may want to get out of a market that's getting smaller.

Market growth = difference between size of old and new market ÷ size of old market x 100%

E.g. if the confectionery market is worth £2 million in 2007, and £4 million in 2008, market growth = £2 000 000 ÷ £2 000 000 x 100 = 100%

As well as size, share and growth, market analysis takes into account things like **profitability** and the **costs** of buying equipment and training staff so you can get into the market (entry costs).

Demand *affects* Market Size, Share *and* Growth

Businesses try to increase their market share by increasing **demand** for their products among consumers. If demand for their products increases, they'll sell more products and make bigger profits. Several factors affect demand — some of these can be controlled by the business, but others can't. The main factors affecting demand are:

1) The **price of the product**. As the price rises, demand tends to go down — as the price falls, demand goes up.

2) The **actions of competitors**. When one manufacturer increases its prices, demand for **cheaper competitor products** tends to **rise**.

3) **Customer income**. When people have **more money to spend**, there's more demand.

4) **Seasonality** — e.g. the demand for ice cream is greater in the **summer**.

5) **Marketing** — successful marketing stimulates demand.

The market was small. But if you will insist on trying to sell belly button fluff...

Understanding Markets

Markets are Segmented into groups of Similar Customers for analysis

Businesses use marketing to find out what customers **need and want**, and to try to convince them to buy their products. Different groups of customers have different needs and wants. **Analysing** different parts (**segments**) of a market allows a business to **focus** on the needs of **specific groups** within a target market. Segmentation can be done by:

1) **Income**, e.g. Chanel make-up is aimed at customers with **high incomes**, and Tesco's own-brand make-up is aimed at lower-income customers. **Luxury products** are usually aimed at high income groups.

2) **Socio-economic class**, e.g. businesses can segment their market based on the kind of **jobs** people have — e.g. **electronic organisers** are aimed at **senior professionals** with busy schedules.

3) **Age**, e.g. firms often target products at specific **age groups** — e.g. 'Sugar' magazine is aimed at teenagers.

4) **Gender**, e.g. chocolate companies aim some products at **women** (e.g. Flake) and some at **men** (e.g. Yorkie®).

5) **Geographical region**, e.g. the core market for **Irn-Bru** is **Scotland**.

6) **Amount of use**, e.g. mobile phone suppliers market **differently** to heavy users and light users.

7) **Ethnic grouping**, e.g. new **ethnic minority** TV channels make it easier for businesses to target **advertising** at particular ethnic groups.

8) **Family size**, e.g. large "**family packs**" of breakfast cereal, loo roll, etc. are aimed at large families. New houses are built with a number of bedrooms to suit the **target customer**.

9) **Lifestyle**, e.g. busy **young workers** might tend to buy lots of microwaveable ready-meals, so a company making **ready-meals** might target this market segment.

All these methods focus on a **characteristic of the customer**. Businesses can also segment markets according to the **reason** for buying a product — as an essential, to cheer yourself up, as a gift, etc. Segmentation is useful for **identifying** potential new **customers**, new **markets**, and the best way of **marketing** a product, but it also has **disadvantages**, e.g.:

1) It can cause a firm to **ignore** the **needs** of other **potential customers**, e.g. if they target a chocolate bar at one particular gender.

2) It can be **difficult** to break the market into **obvious segments**. For example, it is hard to place consumers of washing up liquid into clear categories.

3) Even if a business knows which segments of the market are likely to be interested in its product, it might not know how to **target** its **marketing** to reach them — e.g. how could it target single dads over the age of 40?

Marketing is a Continual Process

1) Businesses start by deciding on **marketing objectives** — figuring out what they want to **achieve** in terms of **sales**.

2) Firms plan **marketing strategies** to achieve their objectives. They **decide** which marketing **activities** to do, based on their **research** and **analysis**.

3) They put their **strategies** into **action** and carry out **marketing activities**, e.g. advertising campaigns.

4) They **monitor sales** to make sure their marketing strategies are having the **right effect**.

5) They **change and improve** their marketing **strategies** and **activities** — if they **need** to.

Practice Questions

Answer on p. 77.

Q1 Name the three most important market conditions that a business can choose to analyse.

Q2 If a business sells 30 000 televisions and the total number of televisions sold is 150 000, what is its market share?

Q3 What is "market segmentation"?

Q4 How can a business make sure its marketing strategies are having the right effect?

Exam Questions

Q1 Outline how a business might estimate its market size and its market share. (4 marks)

Q2 Discuss how a retailer of women's clothing, such as Next, might segment their market. (6 marks)

Did you know — agoraphobia is literally "fear of the marketplace"...

...and although there are lots of different kinds of market out there, you don't need to be frightened of any of them, cos' your mum probably does the shopping anyway. Marketing's about knowing your market, knowing what people want, and knowing how to sell it to them. And to know all this stuff, you've got to do a bit of analysis to find out what's going on.

Market Research

Market research is the collection and analysis of market information such as customer likes and dislikes. It's especially important before starting a new business or launching a new product — it helps prevent disastrous errors.

Market Research is done for Three Main Reasons

1) It helps businesses **spot opportunities**. Businesses research **customer buying patterns** to help them predict what people will be buying in the future. A business might use **research** to help them spot growing markets to get into — and declining markets to get out of. Research on customer likes and dislikes might show a gap in the market.

2) It helps them **work out what to do next**. Businesses research before launching a product or advertising campaign.

3) It helps them see if their **plans are working**. A business that keeps a keen eye on sales figures will notice if their marketing strategy is having the right effect.

> Market research can be **expensive**. **Bad market research** can lead to **disastrous business decisions**. Businesses need to **plan carefully** to make sure they get the **maximum benefit** from market research.

There's Quantitative and Qualitative market research

1) Quantitative research produces **numerical statistics** — facts and figures. It often uses multiple-choice **questionnaires** that ask questions like: "When did you last buy this product? A: within the last day, B: within the last week, C: within the last month, D: within the last year, E: longer ago, F: have never bought this product." These are called **closed questions** because they have **fixed**, **predetermined** answers.

2) Qualitative research looks into the **feelings** and **motivations** of consumers. It uses **focus groups** that have in-depth discussions on a product, and asks questions like: "How does this product make you feel?" These are called **open questions**. The answer isn't restricted to multiple-choice options.

Closed questions (ones with 'yes' or 'no' answers) make analysis easier, but sometimes open questions give more informative data.

There's Primary and Secondary market research

Primary market research is where a business **gathers new data** (or employs someone to do it on their behalf). **Secondary market research** is done by **analysing data** that's already available.

Primary Research

1) Primary data is gathered with **questionnaires, interviews**, post / phone / internet **surveys, focus groups** (e.g. a group of well-informed people) and by observation (e.g. looking at CCTV to see how people shop in stores). Businesses do **test marketing** — e.g. they launch a product in one **region** and measure **sales** and **customer response** before launching it across the country.

2) Primary research uses **sampling** to make predictions about the **whole market** based on a sample (see p.13).

3) Primary data is needed to find out what consumers think of a **new product** or **advert**. You can't use secondary data because, erm, there won't be any secondary data on a brand new product.

4) Primary data is **specific** to the purpose it's needed for. This is great for **niche markets** — secondary data might be too broad or too mainstream to tell you anything useful.

5) Primary data is **exclusive** to the business who commissioned the research, so **competitors can't benefit** from it.

6) Primary research is always **up to date**.

7) **But**, primary research is **labour-intensive, expensive** and **slow**.

Secondary Research

1) **Internal sources** of data include loyalty cards, feedback from company salesmen and analysis of company sales reports, financial accounts, and stock records.

2) **External sources** include government publications like the Social Trends report, marketing agency reports, pressure groups and trade magazines.

3) **Secondary data** is much **easier, faster** and **cheaper** to get hold of than primary data.

4) **But**, secondary data that was gathered for a different purpose might be **unsuitable**. It may contain **errors** and it may be **out of date**.

5) Secondary data is often used to get an **initial understanding** of a market. A business may then do more specific primary research to investigate any **issues** or problems that are shown up by the secondary data.

Market Research

Market researchers need a Representative Sample

1) Market researchers can't ask the **whole** of a **market** to fill in a survey. They select a sample.

2) The sample should try to **represent** the market. It must have **similar proportions** of people in terms of things like age, income, class, ethnicity and gender. If the sample isn't representative, you've got **problems**. However, it isn't always easy to get a representative sample.

3) A **big sample** has a better **chance** of being representative than a **small sample** — but even a big sample won't necessarily be 100% representative. There's always a **margin of error**.

4) The **size** of the **sample** may depend on how many people a **company** can **afford** to ask. If the **cash** available for research is **limited**, the **risk** of the information being **inaccurate** increases.

5) The **size** of the **sample** and the **sampling method** is also affected by the **type** of product or business, the **risk** involved and the **target market**. E.g. a company producing wedding dresses won't use random sampling (see below) as men don't form part of their target market. They're more likely to use quota sampling instead.

> There are **three** main types of sample:
>
> 1) **Simple Random Sample** — Names are picked **randomly** from a list (usually from the electoral register).
>
> 2) **Stratified Sample** — The population is divided into groups and people are selected randomly from each group. The number of people picked from each group is **proportional** to the size of the group.
>
> 3) **Quota Sample** — People are picked who fit into a **category** (e.g. mums between 30 and 40). Businesses use quota sampling to get opinions from the people the product is directly targeted at.

Market research needs to Avoid Bias

The quality of decisions made using market research is only as good as the **accuracy** of the research.

1) Researchers have to be careful to avoid any possible **bias**.

2) Questionnaires and interviews should avoid **leading questions** — questions that are phrased in a way that **leads** the respondent to give a particular answer, e.g "You do like chocolate, don't you?"

3) Interviews suffer from "**interviewer effects**". This is when the **response** isn't what the interviewee **really thinks**. This can be caused by the **personality** of the interviewer — their **opinions** can **influence** the interviewee.

4) Interviewers should only ask for personal data at the **end** of an interview so that they aren't influenced by knowing the **age** or **social background** of the interviewee.

5) The more **representative** a sample is, the more **confidence** a business can have in the results of the research.

Not Spending enough on market research increases the Risk

1) **Market research** can be very expensive. Small businesses don't usually have a lot of money to spend — they may think that research is a waste of money, and spend their cash on fine-tuning the product instead.

2) Not doing enough market research before starting a business **increases the risk** that it will **fail** — businesses don't stand much chance of getting the product right if they **don't know** whether it's really what the market **wants**.

3) It's much less risky to do market research **before** finalising the details of a product or service. Research may tell a firm that they have to seriously **adapt** and **develop** their original idea to make it **fit in** with what the market **needs**.

Practice Questions

Q1 A toy company is researching the market for a new board game.
Write three open and three closed questions that they could use in a consumer survey.

Q2 List two internal and two external sources of secondary data.

Q3 Give three reasons why firms carry out market research.

Q4 What are the three main types of sample, and what are the differences between them?

Exam Question

Q1 Discuss why a new business might pay a market research company to gather primary research for them. (8 marks)

Surveys show that most people lie in surveys...

Research takes time and costs money — businesses must make sure the data's accurate or it'll be as much use as a chocolate fireguard. They also have to actually use the findings to provide what their customers want. If a business can use market research to increase their sales and profits, the market research will pay for itself. Everyone's a winner.

Legal Structure of Businesses

If you're setting up your own business you need to choose a legal structure for it — each type of structure has benefits and drawbacks. It's quite complicated but the next few pages will help you work out what's what.

Sole Trader Businesses are run by an Individual

1) A sole trader is an **individual** trading in his or her own name, or under a suitable trading name. Sole traders are **self-employed**, for example as shopkeepers, plumbers, electricians, hairdressers or consultants.

2) The essential feature of this type of business is that the sole trader has **full responsibility** for the **financial control** of his or her own business and for meeting **running costs** and **capital requirements**. Having full responsibility for all the **debts** of the business is called **unlimited liability**.

3) There are **minimal legal formalities** — the trader simply has to start trading. However, if the business isn't run under the **proprietor's** (owner's) name, the trader has to **register** the company name under the Business Names Act (1985).

'Capital' just means 'money'. 'Capital requirement' is money invested to set up a business or fund growth.

4) There are several **advantages** of being a sole trader:

- **Freedom** — the sole trader is his or her **own boss** and has complete **control** over decisions.
- **Profit** — the sole trader is entitled to **all the profit** made by the business.
- **Simplicity** — there's **less form-filling** than for a limited company. Bookkeeping is less complex.
- **Savings on fees** — there aren't any legal costs like you'd get with drawing up a partnership agreement or limited company documentation.

5) There are **disadvantages** too:

- **Risk** — there's **no one** to **share the responsibilities** of running the business with.
- **Time** — sole traders often need to **work long hours** to meet tight deadlines.
- **Expertise** — the sole trader may have **limited skills** in areas such as finance.
- **Vulnerability** — there's **no cover** if the trader **gets ill** and can't work.
- **Unlimited liability** — the sole trader is **responsible** for all the debts of the business.

A Partnership is a Group of Individuals working together

1) Examples of partnerships include groups of doctors, dentists, accountants and solicitors.

2) The law allows a partnership to have between **two** and **twenty partners**, although some **professions**, e.g. accountants and solicitors, are allowed **more** than twenty.

3) A partnership can either trade in the **names** of the partners, or under a suitable **trading name**.

4) Partnerships need rules. Most partnerships operate according to the terms of a **partnership agreement** (also called a **deed of partnership**). This is a document drawn up by a **solicitor** which sets out:

- The amount of **capital** contributed by each partner.
- The procedure in case of **partnership disputes**.
- How the **profit** will be shared between partners.
- Partners' **voting rights**.
- The procedures for **bringing in new partners** and old partners retiring.

There are **advantages** to a partnership:

1) More owners bring **more capital** to invest at start-up.
2) Partners can bring **more ideas** and **expertise** to a partnership.
3) Partners can **cover** for each other's **holidays** and **illness**.

There are **disadvantages** to a partnership:

1) Partners still have **unlimited liability**.
2) Each partner is liable for **decisions** made by **other partners** — even if they had **no say** in the decision.
3) There's a **risk** of **conflict** between partners.

Legal Structure of Businesses

Liability to pay off Business Debts can be Limited or Unlimited

Sole traders and partnerships have unlimited liability

1) The **business** and the **owner** are **seen as one** under the **law**.

2) This means **business debts** become the **personal debts** of the owner. Sole traders and partners can be forced to **sell personal assets** like their **house** to pay off business debts.

3) Unlimited liability is a **huge financial risk** — it's an important factor to consider when deciding on the type of ownership for a new business.

When Louise's clothes-designing business failed, unlimited liability became a real pain.

Limited liability is a much smaller risk

1) Limited liability means that the owners **aren't personally responsible** for the debts of the business.

2) The **shareholders** of both **private** and **public limited companies** (see p.16) have limited liability, because a limited company has a **separate legal identity** from its owners.

3) The **most** the shareholders in a limited company can lose is the money they have **invested** in the company.

In a limited company, the shareholders own the business.

The difference between limited liability and unlimited liability is **really important**. E.g. a builder puts **£1500** into their own business. The business hits bad times, and eventually goes bankrupt, owing **£20 000**. If the owner is a **sole trader**, he or she is liable to pay the **full amount**. If they're a **shareholder** of a limited company, they only lose the **£1500** they put in.

Some Partners in a partnership can have Limited Liability

1) The Limited Partnership Act (1907) allows a **partnership** to claim **limited liability** for **some** of its partners.

2) The partners with limited liability are called **sleeping partners**.

3) Sleeping partners can put **money** into the partnership but they **aren't allowed** to do anything to **run** the business.

4) There must be at least one **general partner** who **is fully liable** for all **debts** and obligations of the partnership.

Practice Questions

Q1 What legal requirements does a sole trader have to fulfil before he or she can start trading?

Q2 What's the maximum number of partners allowed in a dental practice?

Q3 What's the difference between limited liability and unlimited liability?

Q4 Which represents the biggest risk to the owners of a business — limited liability or unlimited liability?

Q1 Under what circumstances can partners in a partnership have limited liability?

Exam Question

Q1 Eric, a plumber trading as a sole trader, wants to go into partnership with his friend Sandra (also a plumber). Explain why he might want to change the type of ownership of his business? Evaluate the implications of doing so. (6 marks)

Sole traders — they're not just shoemakers...

...They can also be plumbers, window cleaners, greengrocers... You get the idea. The important thing to remember here is that sole traders and partnerships both have unlimited liability, so if you're going to set up one of these types of businesses you need to be pretty sure that it's not going to fail. Otherwise you're in big trouble...cos debts don't mind getting personal.

Legal Structure of Businesses

Companies are different from sole traders and partnerships. They have limited liability for a start.

There are two kinds of Limited Liability Companies — Ltds and PLCs

1) There are **private limited companies** and **public limited companies**.

2) Public and private limited companies have **limited liability** (see p.15).

3) They're owned by **shareholders** and run by **directors**.

More on shares on p.19.

4) The **capital value** (see p.14 for the meaning of capital) of the company is divided into **shares** — these can be **bought** and **sold** by shareholders.

5) Both require a **minimum** of **two shareholders**, and there's **no upper limit** on the number of shareholders.

Private Limited Companies	Public Limited Companies
Can't sell shares to the public. People in the company own all the shares.	Can sell shares to the **public**. They must issue a **prospectus** to inform people about the company before they buy.
Don't have share prices quoted on **stock exchanges**.	Their share prices can be quoted on the **Stock Exchange**.
Shareholders may not be able to sell their shares without the **agreement** of the **other shareholders**.	Shares are **freely transferable** and can be bought and sold through stockbrokers, banks and share shops.
They're often **small** family businesses.	They usually start as private companies and then **go public** later to raise more capital.
There's **no minimum share capital** requirement.	They need **over £50 000** of share capital, and if they're listed on a stock exchange, **at least 25%** of this must be publicly available. People in the company can own the rest of the shares.
They end their name with the word "limited" or **Ltd**.	They always end their name with the initials **PLC**.

Companies are governed by the Companies Act (1985)

The Companies Act (1985) says that two important documents must be drawn up **before** a company can start trading. These are the **memorandum of association** and the **articles of association**.

Memorandum of Association

1) The **memorandum of association** gives the company name followed by **Ltd**, if it's a private limited company, or **PLC**, if it's a public limited company, and it gives the company's business address.

2) The Memorandum of Association says what the **objectives** of the company are.

3) It gives **details** of the company's capital, e.g. £250 000 divided into 250 000 Ordinary Shares of £1 each.

4) It states clearly that the **shareholders' liability is limited**.

Articles of Association

1) The **articles of association** are the **internal rules** of the company.

2) They give the **names** of the **directors**.

3) They say **how directors are appointed** and what kind of **power** they have.

4) The articles of association say what the **shareholders' voting rights** are.

5) They set out when and how the company will hold **shareholders' meetings**.

6) The articles of association set out how the company will **share** its **profits**.

Companies House is where records of all UK companies are kept.

The **memorandum of association** and **articles of association** must both be sent to **Companies House**.
The Registrar of Companies issues a **certificate of incorporation** so that the company can start trading.
Once it's up and running, the company is legally obliged to produce **annual reports** of its financial activities.

Companies are controlled by Shareholders and Directors

1) All the shareholders in a **small** private limited company are usually the **directors**. The shareholders who hold the **most shares** have the **most power**.

2) In larger private limited companies, directors are **elected** to the board by **shareholders**. The board makes the important decisions. **Shareholders vote** on the performance of the board at the Annual General Meeting (**AGM**).

3) Shares in a PLC can be owned by **anyone**. The people who **own** the company (the shareholders) don't necessarily **control** the company — it's **controlled** by the **directors**. This is called the "**divorce of ownership and control**".

Legal Structure of Businesses

Not-for-Profit businesses are another type of business structure

1) As their name suggests, not-for-profit businesses are **not** set up to make a **profit**. Instead, they have other aims, often to **help** people in need or benefit the community.

2) **Not-for-profit** businesses are run in a similar way to other businesses. They usually have money coming into and going out of the business — the main difference is that the money generated by the business **doesn't** go to the owners or shareholders as **profit**.

3) **Public-sector** organisations providing free services to the public are not-for-profit businesses. NHS hospitals are one example — their aim is to provide healthcare rather than to make a profit. The NHS and other organisations like UK police forces and the fire service are run in a similar way to other businesses, but they don't charge for their services so they don't make a profit — they are funded by the UK **tax system**.

4) **Charities** like the Red Cross, Oxfam and Amnesty International are also not-for-profit businesses — they make money from **donations** and business activities (like charity shops), but this money is used to fund charitable activities, e.g. setting up hospitals in developing countries. Charities get **tax reductions** because of their not-for-profit structure.

5) Many **local organisations** and societies are also run as not-for-profit businesses — e.g. amateur theatre groups might charge for tickets to see their performances, but the money generated from ticket sales is put back into the business, e.g. to cover the costs of renting a building for the performance, buying costumes, etc.

Entrepreneurs have to Choose a Legal Structure for their business

1) When someone sets up a business, they have to **decide** whether to set up as a sole trader, a partnership, a private limited company (Ltd.) or a public limited company (PLC). Each of the business structures has **advantages** and **disadvantages** — the entrepreneur has to decide which is most **suitable** for their needs.

2) Setting up a **sole trader** business gives the owner **control** over the business, but **unlimited liability** is a drawback. It's a **simple** way to set up a small business, but there's a lot of **risk** involved for the owner.

3) A **partnership** means more people with more **money** and more **ideas**, but there's a risk of **disagreements** between partners and there's still **unlimited liability**.

4) A **private limited company** (Ltd.) has **limited liability** and the shareholders keep **control** over who other shares are sold to, but it's much more **complicated** to set up than a sole trader business.

5) **Public limited companies** aren't usually a suitable option for new businesses because they need at least **£50 000** of share capital to start with, and most new businesses can't raise that much money.

6) Businesses can **change** their structure — sole traders can join together to form a partnership, or they can become a private limited company if the business is successful and they want to expand. Lots of private limited companies become PLCs when they want to raise more money to **expand** the business. It's much less common, but PLCs can also become private limited companies if they are taken over by a private limited company or if the managers **buy out** the **shareholders**. For example, in 2002, Arcadia Group PLC was taken over by Philip Green's private limited company Taveta Investments Ltd. and is now Arcadia Group Ltd.

Practice Questions

Q1 State two differences between private and public limited companies.

Q2 What are the names of the two documents a company needs to draw up before it can start trading?

Q3 Why are new businesses not usually set up as PLCs?

Q4 Give three examples of not-for-profit businesses.

Exam Question

Q1 Made-Up Organics, a company selling organic make-up and toiletries, is owned by Isabelle Greenberg, a sole trader. The business has been growing over the past few years and she is thinking of becoming a private limited company instead. Discuss the advantages and disadvantages of doing this. (6 marks)

All this legal stuff seemed much more entertaining on Ally McBeal...

It's a bit of a pain having to learn all the legal ins and outs of different business structures, but make sure you do because this is quite likely to crop up in the exam. You might be asked to decide whether a particular business would be better off as a sole trader, partnership, private limited company or PLC, so you need to be able to choose between them.

Financing a New Business

Entrepreneurs need to find finance for their business if they want to turn it from an idea into reality.
There are loads of different sources of finance out there, so it's just a case of choosing the right one.

Lots of **Costs** are involved in starting a new business

1) New businesses **can't** usually **put off** paying costs like employee's wages, rent on business premises and payment for equipment and raw materials. This is a **problem** because money won't start coming into the business until much **later**, when the business starts being **paid** for its products.

2) If the business **can't** pay what it owes in time, it will have to **close down**.

3) To make sure that the business will **survive** until revenue starts coming in, and to pay all the **bills** once the business starts trading, the entrepreneur needs to find a way of **financing** the business.

4) There are several possible ways of financing a new business — they all have **benefits** and **drawbacks**, and are suitable in different **circumstances**. Most businesses use a combination of different sources of finance.

Entrepreneurs can use their **Savings** to finance their business

1) Most entrepreneurs use some of their **own** money to finance their business.

2) Investing some of your own money shows that you have **faith** that the business will be **successful** — this can **encourage** banks to give you a loan or other people to invest in the business.

3) Not many entrepreneurs will have enough savings to cover **all** the money they need to start up their business — most need to find **additional** sources of finance too.

The types of finance available to a business depend on what kind of business it is — not all types of finance are suitable for all types of firm.

Entrepreneurs can take out **Loans** to finance their business

1) Entrepreneurs can get **loans** from **banks** to finance their business. They borrow a fixed amount of **money** and pay it back over a fixed period of **time** with **interest** — the amount they have to pay back depends on the interest rate and the length of time the loan is for.

2) Banks need **security** for a loan, usually in the form of property.

3) Loans are a good way of financing the **start-up** of a business and paying for **assets** like machinery and computers. They are **not** a good way to cover the **day-to-day** running costs of the business.

Advantages of bank loans

1) You're **guaranteed** the money for the duration of the loan (the bank can't suddenly demand it back).

2) You only have to pay back the **loan** and **interest** — the bank won't **own** any of your business and you don't have to give them a share of the **profits**.

3) The interest charges for a loan are usually **lower** than for an overdraft.

Disadvantages of bank loans

1) They can be **difficult** to arrange because the bank will only lend the entrepreneur money if they think they are going to get it back. If the entrepreneur doesn't own any property or other assets that can be used for security, they might not be able to get a loan.

2) Keeping up with the **repayments** can be difficult if cash isn't coming into the business quickly enough. The entrepreneur might **lose** whatever the loan is secured on (e.g. their home) — the bank can sell it to get their money back.

3) The entrepreneur might have to pay a **charge** if they decide to pay the loan back **early**.

Entrepreneurs may also be able to borrow money from **friends** or **family** — they will probably charge **less interest** than banks, or even none at all. They're also unlikely to ask for security for the loan, and might be more **flexible** about when repayments are made. However, if the business fails then the lender will **lose** the money that they lent to the entrepreneur — this could have a very negative effect on the **relationship** between the entrepreneur and the lender.

Financing a New Business

Entrepreneurs can use *Overdrafts* to finance their business

1) **Overdrafts** are where a bank lets a business spend **more** money **than** it **has** in its account, up to a **limit**. The overspend is recorded as a **negative** figure.

2) Many businesses use overdrafts to cover some of their day-to-day costs, especially if they have **short-term** cash flow problems (see p.30-31). They're **not** suitable for **long-term** finance though.

Advantages of overdrafts

1) They're **quick** and **easy** to set up — banks will usually offer them to anyone, unlike loans.

2) They're **flexible** — the business can borrow any amount up to the overdraft limit, and only has to pay interest on the amount that it borrows.

Disadvantages of overdrafts

1) The interest rate is usually very **high** so they are **expensive** if they're used over long periods of time.

2) The bank can **remove** the overdraft facility at any time and demand all the money back.

Limited companies can sell *Shares* to raise finance

1) If the business is set up as a **private limited company**, the entrepreneur can finance it using **ordinary share capital** — money raised by selling **shares** in the business.

2) Entrepreneurs can sell shares to their **friends** and **family**, or to **venture capitalists** — professional investors who buy shares in new businesses that they think have the potential to be successful.

3) The drawback of selling shares rather than taking out a loan is that the entrepreneur no longer **owns** all of the business — they have to give the shareholders a share of the **profits**, and they also have to give them a **say** in how the business is run.

Sally tried using her feminine wiles, but nothing could persuade Steve to buy shares in her suede raincoat business.

Practice Questions

Q1 Explain why a new business needs finance.
Q2 What is the main drawback of borrowing money from friends and family?
Q3 What is the difference between an overdraft and a loan?
Q4 What is meant by the term "venture capitalist"?

Exam Questions

Q1 Suggest what type of finance might be suitable for financing the launch of a cybercafé business. (6 marks)

Q2 Discuss the advantages and disadvantages of financing a new business using a bank loan. (8 marks)

Unfortunately you can't sell shares in being slightly bored with BS...

I was planning on financing my business with £1 coins from the back of the sofa. Guess not, then. All kidding aside, it's worth knowing about the different kinds of finance that entrepreneurs can use to start up their business. Learn what types of finance are suitable for the short- and long-term running of a firm too and you'll be laughing if it comes up in the exam.

Location

When you're deciding where to set up a business, it's all about location, location, location.

Businesses use **Cost-Benefit Analysis** to choose a **Location**

1) **Cost-benefit analysis** means **weighing** up the **costs** of an opportunity against its potential **benefits**.

2) Renting or buying somewhere is a big **investment** for a business. When deciding where to locate, businesses consider how each location will affect **costs** and **revenues** (e.g. rents and labour costs in Newcastle are likely to be lower than rents and labour costs in London). Businesses use **quantitative analysis** techniques such as **break-even analysis** to measure this (see p. 28-29).

3) Businesses calculate how many sales they'll need to break even at each potential location. Where the **costs of operating** from a location are **high**, the **break-even output** will be higher. It's better to put your business where break-even output is low.

Businesses make **Location** decisions based on **Practical** factors

The best location for a business depends on several factors, and is different for different types of business.

Transport costs affect where businesses are located

1) **Manufacturing** businesses which provide **bulky finished products** should be located near to their **customers** to cut down on distribution costs. Bulky products made from **lightweight** components are called "**bulk increasing**" goods.

2) Other products need **bulky raw materials** to make a **lightweight end product** — these are "**bulk decreasing**" goods. They need to be located near the source of **raw materials** to keep transport costs down.

3) A good **transport infrastructure** (see below) cuts distribution costs.

4) **Services** don't have large distribution costs. Decisions on where to locate services are based mainly on other criteria.

> E.g. <u>beer</u> — made of <u>water</u> (available anywhere), plus hops and barley (<u>low in bulk</u> compared to the <u>finished</u> product). Breweries tend to be located near <u>consumers</u> and <u>transport infrastructure</u>, not near hop or barley fields.

> E.g. a small business producing bottled <u>mineral water</u> is likely to be based near the <u>source</u> of the water — otherwise it would be very <u>expensive</u> to transport the water to the bottling factory.

A good location needs a good infrastructure

1) Business organisations benefit from access to **motorways**, fast **rail** links, **sea ports** and **airports**.

2) Transport infrastructure is needed for the **import** of **raw materials**, the **distribution** of **finished products**, and for **staff** to get to work.

3) Businesses also need **support services**. Most business organisations need some form of **commercial** support such as **banking**, **insurance** and **marketing** agencies.

4) Often there's a need for **technical** support such as engineering services and **IT** assistance.

Businesses need a location with good land and labour resources

1) There must be a **good supply** of labour resources in the area where a business will be located.

2) The labour force must also be **suitable** — e.g. they might need to be literate, they might need special skills such as IT, technical knowledge of machinery, etc.

3) The area might need **local training facilities** for staff, e.g. a college or university.

4) The area needs **facilities** such as affordable housing, suitable schooling, medical facilities and retail and leisure outlets to provide a good **quality of life** for staff.

5) Businesses can afford to pay workers less in areas where the **cost of living** is lower. To take full advantage of this, businesses need to locate **overseas** where labour costs are far lower than in the UK.

6) Businesses also need the right land resources. They might need to **expand** in the future.

7) The **cost** of **land** and **property** for factories and business premises varies significantly from area to area — land in the London area is far more expensive than land in mid-Wales, for example.

8) **International** location decisions must take account of variations in the cost of water and **electricity**.

Location decisions depend on the market

1) Some businesses such as **retailers** need to locate **near customers**, in order to catch the passing trade.

Location

The Government provides Incentives to locate in certain areas

Governments usually want to attract businesses to areas with high **unemployment**.

1) In 1998, the UK government set up 8 **Regional Development Agencies** (RDAs) to coordinate and encourage development. They can provide **financial assistance** to businesses through grants, loans and equity (share) investment. They provide **financial** and **management advice**, and can help businesses find the right location.

2) They can provide **financial assistance** to business through grants, loans and equity (share) investment. They also provide **financial guidance** and **management support**.

3) They can also help businesses find the right **location**.

4) As another part of its regional policy, the UK government has named certain economically less-developed parts of the country as **assisted areas**. In these areas government **grants** are available to persuade manufacturing and service businesses to locate there. Cornwall and the Scottish Highlands are two examples of assisted areas.

> The government often use "**carrots**" and "**sticks**" to encourage businesses to locate in deprived areas.
> E.g. a "**carrot**" would be a **grant** given to a business locating in an area of high unemployment.
> A "**stick**" would be **refusing planning permission** to build a factory in an area where there are already lots of jobs.

There are also Qualitative Factors involved in Choosing a Location

1) Decisions about where to base a business are not always just based on things that can be **measured**.

2) Entrepreneurs might choose to start a business near where they **live** — e.g. Dyson™ is based in Wiltshire, near the owner and inventor's home.

3) Some places have a **good image** which suits the image of the product. High fashion works better in London or Paris than in Scunthorpe or Workington — London and Paris already have a fashionable image.

Businesses don't usually find an Ideal Location

1) All these factors rarely, if ever, combine in one place to create an **ideal** location. It's more likely that the decision of where to locate a business is based on a **compromise** between different factors.

2) The **importance** of each factor depends on the **type** of business. A coffee shop needs to prioritise being near its customers, but a top restaurant might cut costs by locating in a rural area, because people will travel to eat there.

3) Small businesses don't usually have much **choice** about which area of the country to locate in — entrepreneurs don't usually have spare cash to move location, so they tend to set up the business in the area where they already live. They still have to decide whereabouts in the town/city to locate — e.g. someone thinking of opening a coffee shop might choose to set up close to a university to attract students.

4) Small businesses can be at a **disadvantage** because they might not be able to afford the best location — e.g. an entrepreneur setting up a clothes shop might not be able to afford the rent in the city centre, so their shop might be in a side street where fewer people pass by.

5) **Modern technology** means that many businesses can be more **flexible** about their location. Businesses that trade over the internet rather than face-to-face can be based anywhere in the country. Doing business over the internet can be a useful way for entrepreneurs who don't live in big cities to reach customers.

Practice Questions

Q1 Identify and briefly explain three factors which affect location cost.

Q2 What are assisted areas?

Q3 Why is it difficult for small businesses to find an ideal location?

Exam Question

Q1 Discuss the factors that an entrepreneur should consider when deciding where to locate a restaurant business. (10 marks)

Phil and Kirstie can't help you now...

You're going to have to learn the factors which affect business location, no maybes about it. If this comes up in the exam (more than likely) you'll probably get a case study with some facts and figures about a business, and you'll be asked to say why the business chose to locate where it did. Or you might have to write a report recommending a location for a business.

Employing People

Even the most brilliant entrepreneurs can't do all the work themselves — they're going to need to take on more staff at some point. But there are more options than just taking on full-time employees, so sorting out staffing can be tricky.

Small businesses need to *Consider* their *Staffing Needs*

Small businesses might need to increase or decrease their staffing levels in the following situations:

1) The business is **expanding** — businesses may need **extra staff** to cope with the increased workload.

2) **Demand** increases — **extra staff** might be needed so that the business can keep up with demand.

3) A change in **direction** — if a business decides to move into a new area (e.g. if a hair salon decides to start providing beauty treatments), new staff with new **expertise** might be required.

4) **Quiet periods** — having too high staff levels at these times can cause problems for a small business because they have to **pay** all their staff even if they don't really need them.

Staff can be *Full-Time* or *Part-Time*

Most small businesses employ mainly **full-time** staff (staff working 35 hours or more per week). However, full-time staff are not always the best option for small businesses. Employing **part-time** staff can be better in some circumstances:

Advantages of part-time staff

1) Employing part-time staff can **save** the business **money**. There's no point paying full-time staff to be at work all week if there's not enough work for them to do.

2) Businesses have more **flexibility** to manage **workloads** — the business can use part-time workers to cover times when the workload is greater due to higher demand.

3) Part-time staff may have a better **work/life balance** (a good split between working for money and leisure time), so they are less likely to take time off with stress, or take sick days. Employing part-time staff to deal with increased workloads also eases the **pressure** on full-time staff, so stress and absenteeism among full-time staff are also likely to be reduced.

4) A better work/life balance is likely to mean **happier** staff — this could lead to an increase in **productivity**.

5) There is a wider range of **skills** among the workforce — by increasing the number of employees the business increases its pool of skills and experience.

Disadvantages of part-time staff

1) It can be difficult to **find** good part-time workers because most jobseekers are likely to be looking for **full-time** work.

2) Part-time employees can sometimes be less **dedicated** and **loyal** than full-time workers — they spend a lower proportion of their time working for the business so it's not such an important part of their life.

3) Part-time employees spend less time working for the business so they might not have as much **experience** of how the business works as full-time staff do.

4) The recruitment and training processes are **time-consuming** and **expensive** — it's only worth spending money on hiring part-time employees if you're sure they're going to save you money.

1) It's important for small businesses to get the **balance** between part-time and full-time staff **right** — e.g. an entrepreneur who sets up a small clothes shop might employ one full-time member of staff, and a part-time member of staff to work on Fridays and Saturdays, when the shop is busiest.

2) When entrepreneurs start up new businesses, they might be **unsure** of how **busy** they are likely to be, or how many employees they'll need to cope with **demand** — it's usually best to take on **part-time** staff until they are sure that demand will be high enough to need full-time workers.

3) **Job-sharing** is when two (or more) employees work **part-time** sharing the **same** job. They usually work on different days of the week or alternate weeks, and they share the responsibility and pay of the job. This can be a good way of allowing higher-level staff like **managers** to work part-time without disrupting the business' activities, although it needs careful planning.

Laura found balancing crockery on her feet much easier than balancing her staffing levels.

Employing People

Staff can be *Temporary* or *Permanent*

1) **Permanent** staff have an **ongoing contract** to work for a business and a **guaranteed salary**.

2) A business can only stop employing its **permanent staff** by **dismissing** them (if they behave badly or are incapable of doing their job) or making them **redundant** (if the business no longer needs anyone to do their job). It's **expensive** to make permanent employees redundant — the firm has to give them redundancy pay.

3) **Temporary** staff work for the business for a **fixed period** of time (e.g. 6 months) or on a **weekly basis** — the business can renew the employee's contract if extra staff are needed for longer than this.

4) A small business can employ **temporary** workers in **high-risk** periods when the business' future is uncertain — then they can easily **reduce** their number of employees without having to pay redundancy money.

5) Recruitment is an **expensive** process, so businesses often use **employment agencies** to find temporary staff — the agency advertises the job and finds a suitable candidate, and the business has to pay a fee to the agency. In this case, workers are employed by the **agency** rather than the business.

6) **Contractors** can be used if a business needs staff with **specialist** skills on a **short-term** basis. Contractors charge a set fee for doing a **specific job** for a limited period of time, and staff are employed by the **contractor** rather than the business. Businesses tend to use contractors for services such as gardening, cleaning, building work, IT support and security.

Attracting new employees is *Difficult*

1) Businesses invest a lot of time and money in recruiting staff, so it's important to find the right employees.

2) It's hard for small businesses to find good employees because they have limited resources to spend on recruitment — e.g. advertising jobs in national newspapers and magazines may be the best way to reach the best potential employees, but it may be too expensive for a small business.

3) Small businesses also find it difficult to attract good candidates because they cannot offer the same salaries and benefits as larger companies with more resources.

4) Businesses also have to consider legal issues when recruiting new staff. It's illegal for businesses to discriminate against potential employees because of their age, gender, race, religion, sexual orientation or because they have a disability. If a business refused to employ someone on these grounds, candidates could take them to an employment tribunal, and the business might have to pay compensation.

Businesses can get *Advice* on *Employment Matters*

1) Getting staffing **wrong** causes big **problems** for small businesses — if they don't have **enough** staff they won't be able to meet **demand**, and **too many** staff will create unnecessary **costs** for the business.

2) It's useful for small businesses to get expert **advice** on employment — small businesses can get **free** advice from Business Link or the Small Business Advisor at their bank.

3) Business owners who are members of the British Chambers of Commerce, the Federation of Small Businesses or the Institute of Directors can get expert employment advice — there's a membership **fee** for joining though.

4) Businesses can also **pay** specialist **consultants** to advise them, but this is an **expensive** option for small businesses.

Practice Questions

Q1 Give three examples of situations that might require businesses to consider their staffing needs.
Q2 State two advantages and two disadvantages of part-time staff.
Q3 Name three potential sources of advice on employment matters.

Exam Question

Q1 Discuss the practical and legal difficulties for small businesses of finding and attracting good employees. (10 marks)

You could always employ a lookalike to sit the exam for you...

Finding the right employees might be stressful for entrepreneurs, but it shouldn't be too much of a headache for you — as long as you make sure that you know the difference between part-time, full-time, permanent and temporary staff, and learn the advantages and disadvantages of each, you'll be able to sail through any employment questions that pop up in the exam.

Business Plans

*Making a plan is one of the keys to business success. If you want your business to work,
you've got to be prepared — any boy scout'll tell you that.*

A **Business Plan** sets out the **Objectives** of the business

A business plan is a document that states **what** the owner(s) want to do and **how** they intend to do it.
There are several reasons for writing a business plan before starting a business:

1) The main purpose of a business plan is usually to get financial backing for the business. A business
plan shows the **financial risk** involved in setting up the business — this is important for potential
lenders or **investors** who may want to help finance the start-up. Banks and venture capitalists will want
to see a business plan before they'll think about investing.

2) Setting down all the plans for the business in a report helps the entrepreneur to assess the business'
strengths and **weaknesses**, and allows them to see whether their idea is actually **realistic**. It also allows
them to identify areas that they need to think about and plan more thoroughly.

3) The business plan is an important **management** tool — it gives details of business **objectives**, which the
entrepreneur can compare with the **actual** performance of the business once it starts trading in order
to track its progress. It also reminds the owner of the **ideas** they had before the business started.

Business plans are divided into **Sections**

Most business plans contain the following sections:

1) **Executive summary** — a general **overview** of the business which contains the **key points** from all the other
sections. It's really important because if potential investors aren't impressed by the executive summary then
they might not bother to read the rest of the business plan.

2) **Business summary** — describes what **type** of business the entrepreneur wants to set up, what **product(s)** or
service(s) the business intends to provide, **why** it wants to provide them, and what makes it different from/better
than the competition (its **competitive advantage**). It also includes the **legal structure** of the business, and the
entrepreneur's vision for the **future** of the business.

> E.g. if the type of business is a **cookery school**, the service it offers would be **cookery lessons**,
> and it might also offer products like **recipe books** and **cooking equipment**.
>
> The entrepreneur might want to provide these things because there isn't a cookery school in the area and
> there is **demand** for cooking lessons due to the popularity of TV chefs like Jamie Oliver and Nigella Lawson.
>
> Its **competitive advantage** might be that it can **source** all its fresh **ingredients locally**.
>
> The entrepreneur might be a **sole trader**, or the business could be a **partnership** or **limited company**
>
> The entrepreneur's vision for the **future** might be:
> (a) to have a **revenue** of **£30 000** in the third year of trading,
> (b) to attract customers from all over the **UK** for cooking holidays as well as holding classes for **local** people,
> (c) to eventually open a **bed-and-breakfast** where students on the holiday courses can stay.

3) **Production plan** — sets out **how many** products the business intends to produce, and how it will go about
producing them (e.g. how many workers will be required, what the costs of production will be, etc.).

4) **Marketing plan**, the entrepreneur defines the **market** for the business and explains who its main **competitors**
are, who the **target customers** are and what the product's **unique selling point** is (see p.60). It includes details
of any **market research** that the entrepreneur has done, and any **promotions** that they intend to run.

5) **Human resources plan** — outlines the relevant **qualifications** and **experience** of the entrepreneur and other
people involved in setting up the business. It also sets out how many **employees** the business intends to take on,
and how much it intends to pay them.

6) **Operations plan** — gives details of where the business will be **located**, whether the business will **own** or **rent**
property and machinery, etc.

7) **Financial plan** — covers all of the financial **forecasts** for the business, e.g. how much **capital** they need to
start the business, how they are going to **finance** the business (see p. 18-19), their **break-even** calculations (see
p. 28-29), and a **cash flow forecast** (see p. 30-31). The financial information explains how the business will
survive in the start-up period.

Business Plans

It's **Difficult** to produce an **Accurate** business plan

1) Business plans are **never** 100% accurate because it's **impossible** for a business to get accurate information about costs, revenue, etc. **before** it has started trading.

2) Just because the business plan says that the business should be making a profit of £2000 a month doesn't mean that that's what will actually happen — there's no way of knowing for definite, so there's always **risk** involved in setting up a business.

3) However, producing a thorough business plan **reduces** the risk of the business failing.

Entrepreneurs can get **Advice** on creating a business plan

If only Bryan had taken some professional advice before setting up his cruise business, it might have worked out a lot better.

1) The business plan is **really important**, so entrepreneurs need to get it right.

2) Entrepreneurs can get **free** help and advice on writing a business plan from a government organisation like Business Link, or from the manager or Small Business Advisor at their bank — they can give entrepreneurs sample business plans or CDs that guide you through the process of writing a business plan. Some **websites** also provide sample business plans free of charge, which entrepreneurs can adapt to their own business.

3) Entrepreneurs can also get expert guidance and advice from business consultants or accountants, but this is a more **expensive** option.

Established Businesses produce business plans too

1) Business plans are not just for new start-up businesses — it can also be very useful for **established** businesses to write a new business plan in certain situations.

2) If a business is planning to launch a **new product**, creating a new business plan can allow managers to see whether it is likely to be **profitable**. If not, they might decide not to go ahead with the launch.

3) A new business plan can also be useful if the business is planning to **expand** (e.g. if the owner of a successful restaurant decides to open another branch in a different town), especially since they might need to find external **finance** to do it.

Eilidh's clothes shop was a big success in Dundee, but she'd have saved a lot of money if she'd done a new business plan before she opened the branch in Chelmsford.

Practice Questions

Q1 What is usually the main reason for producing a business plan?

Q2 Why is the executive summary important?

Q3 Give five examples of information that's covered in a business plan.

Q4 Name three sources of expert advice on creating a business plan.

Exam Question

Q1 Explain why every new business should have a business plan. (10 marks)

"Slaps bunnies" and "painless buns" — anagrams of "business plan"...

Business plans are quite simple really — if you're going to open a business it makes sense to plan what you're going to do. Learn the key things a business plan includes, why entrepreneurs need them, and remember that writing an accurate plan for a new firm is always a bit of a problem. An anagram of problem is "lob perm" — which isn't a plan for a new hairdresser...

Costs, Revenues and Profits

Businesses need to know how much their revenue and costs are — otherwise they wouldn't have a clue how much profit they were making. Costs, revenues and profits are all related.

Revenue is the Money a business makes from Sales

1) Revenue is the **value of sales** — it's sometimes just called **sales**, and can also be called **turnover**. It's the amount of money generated by sales of a product, **before** any deductions are made.

2) You can work out the revenue by multiplying the **price** that the customer pays for each item by the **number of items** that the business sells:

> Revenue = selling price per item × quantity of items sold

E.g. if a business sells **2000** teapots for **£8** each, the revenue is £8 × 2000 = **£16 000**.

Costs can be Fixed or Variable

1) **Fixed costs** don't change with output. **Rent** on a factory, business **rates**, **senior managers' salaries** and the cost of **new machinery** are fixed costs. When output increases, a business makes more use of the facilities it's already got. The **cost** of those facilities **doesn't change**.

2) **Variable costs** rise and fall as output changes. Hourly **wages**, **raw material costs** and the **packaging costs** for each product are all variable costs.

3) **Semi-variable costs** have fixed and variable parts. **Telephone bills** are a good example of **semi-variable** costs. Businesses have to pay a **fixed** amount for their phone line plus a **variable** amount depending on the phone calls they've made.

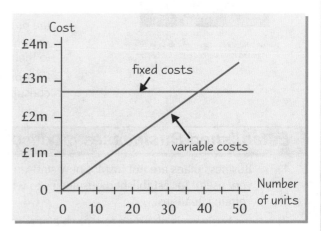

Profit = Revenue – Costs

1) When you deduct the costs from the revenue, what is left is the **profit**.

2) **Net profit** is what you get when you subtract **fixed and variable** costs from revenue — see above for explanations of fixed and variable costs.

For more on profits, see p. 36-37.

E.g. a teapot business has fixed costs of £4000 pcm and variable costs of £4 per teapot. It sells 2000 teapots in one month for £8 each, so its revenue is £16 000. Its variable costs that month are 2000 × £4 = £8000. The **net profit** would be: £16 000 – (£8000 + £4000) = **£4000**.

3) As well as being affected by costs, **revenue** and **profit** are affected by both **sales volume** and **price**. The amount of sales you lose by putting the price up varies — see **price elasticity of demand** on p. 68-69.

4) Businesses can do two things with profits. They can **give them to the shareholders** as dividend payments (sole traders and partnerships usually vary their salary according to how much profit they've made) or they can **re-invest** their profits in new activities.

Cost, revenue and profit were all related.

5) **Shareholders** often want a **short-term** reward for supporting the business. In the long term, it's often better for the business to hold on to the profit and **re-invest** it in future projects.

Costs, Revenues and Profits

Large-Scale Production helps keep costs Low

The more a business produces, the **lower** the **cost per unit** produced. This is because the **fixed costs** are **shared out** between **more items**. The best way to show this is with an example:

1) MicroDave make microwave ovens. The **fixed costs** of running MicroDave are £200 000 per year. The **variable costs** of materials and labour are £15 per microwave.

2) If MicroDave make **5000 microwaves a year**, the total production costs are... £200 000 + (£15 × 5000) = **£275 000**. The **cost per microwave** is £275 000 ÷ 5000 = **£55**.

3) If MicroDave make **20 000 microwaves a year**, the total production costs are... £200 000 + (£15 × 20 000) = **£500 000**. The **cost per microwave** is £500 000 ÷ 20 000 = **£25**.

Businesses use information on Product Costs to Make Decisions

1) Businesses use **cost** information to set the **selling price** of their products and services (see p.28). They set the price to make sure they'll make a **profit**. (Number of sales × price) – costs = profit.

2) If a business is a **"price taker"** in a very competitive market, it **doesn't have control** of the **selling price** of its products — it takes whatever price the market will pay. Businesses in this situation need accurate **costing** information to work out if it's **profitable** to make and sell a product at all. E.g. farmers have to sell milk, carrots, potatoes, etc to supermarkets for whatever price the supermarkets are willing to pay — if they try to put their prices up, supermarkets will just buy from other farmers instead.

3) Businesses set **budgets** (see p.32-33) which forecast how much costs are going to be over a year. Managers need to know what costs they're incurring **now**, so that they can know whether they're **meeting** the budget.

Costs also relate to Missed Opportunities

1) **Opportunity cost** puts a value on a product or business decision in terms of what the business had to give up to have it.

2) Businesses must **choose** where to spend their limited finance. Managers **compare opportunity costs** when making their decisions. The opportunity cost of an advert half way through an episode of X Factor might be five screenings of the same advert in the middle of Emmerdale.

Two cars... or 30 holidays... or 8000 McDonald's Value Meals...

Practice Questions

Q1 What is the formula for calculating revenue?

Q2 Give three examples of a fixed cost.

Q3 How is net profit calculated?

Q4 What is an opportunity cost?

Answer on p.77.

Exam Questions

Q1 Explain what is meant by the term 'variable costs', (2 marks)

Q2 Beth Brook Hats employs two hat-makers, each at £280/week. Beth, as Managing Director, pays herself £400/week. The other fixed costs are £300/week. The variable costs of raw materials are £14 per hat. Hats sell for £50.

(a) Draw a graph to show fixed, variable and total costs for outputs from 0 hats/week to 100 hats/week. (6 marks)

(b) Calculate the profit that Beth is making at her current output level of 60 hats per week, assuming weekly sales match output. (4 marks)

If you don't learn this, it'll cost you...

Costs, revenue and profit are kind of at the heart of this section. They're pretty simple concepts, but they're used to work out everything else, so make sure you get them straight in your head. You need to be able to calculate revenue and profit, so learn the formulas well, and make sure you're clear on the difference between fixed and variable costs too. Oh joy...

Break-Even Analysis

Break-even analysis is a great way of working out how much you need to sell to make a profit.

Breaking Even means Covering your Costs

1) The **break-even point** is the level of sales a business needs to **cover their costs**. At this point, costs = revenue.

2) When sales are **below** the break-even point, costs are more than revenue — the business makes a **loss**.
When sales are **above** the break-even point, revenue exceeds costs — the business makes a **profit**.

3) **New businesses** should always do a **break-even analysis** to **find** the break-even point. It tells them how much they will need to sell to break even. Banks and venture capitalists thinking of **loaning** money to the business will need to **see** a break-even analysis as part of the **business plan**. This helps them to decide whether to lend money to the firm — if they think that the business is unlikely to sell enough to break even, they won't lend their money.

4) **Established businesses** preparing to launch **new products** use break even analysis to work out how much **profit** they are likely to make, and also to predict the impact of the new activity on **cash flow** (see p.30-31).

Contribution is used to work out the Break-Even Output

1) **Contribution** is the difference between the **selling price** of a product and the **variable costs** it takes to produce it.

> **Contribution per unit = selling price per unit – variable costs per unit**

Learn this formula for calculating break-even output

2) Contribution is used to **pay fixed costs**. The amount left over is profit.

3) **The break-even point** is where **contribution = fixed costs**.
Break-even output is fixed costs over contribution per unit.

$$\text{Break-even output} = \frac{\text{fixed costs}}{\text{contribution per unit}}$$

> **Example:** Harry sets up a business to print T-shirts. The **fixed costs** of premises and the T-shirt printers are **£3000**. The **variable costs** per T-shirt (the T-shirt, ink, wages) are **£5**. Each printed T-shirt sells for **£25**.
>
> **Contribution per unit** = £25 – £5 = **£20**
>
> **Break-even output** = £3000 ÷ £20 = **150**   So, Harry has to sell **150** T-shirts to **break even**.

Draw a Break-Even Chart to show the Break-Even Point

1) Break-even charts show **costs** and **revenues** plotted against **output**. Businesses use break-even charts to see how costs and revenues **vary** with different levels of output.

2) **Output** goes on the **horizontal axis**. The scale needs to let you plot output from 0 to the maximum possible.

3) **Costs and revenue** both go on the vertical axis. Use a scale that lets you plot from 0 to the maximum revenue.

4) Plot **fixed** costs. (On the diagram on the right, fixed costs are the blue horizontal line.)

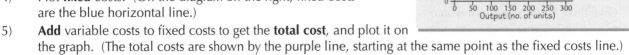

5) **Add** variable costs to fixed costs to get the **total cost**, and plot it on the graph. (The total costs are shown by the purple line, starting at the same point as the fixed costs line.)

6) Next, plot **revenue** (see p.28 for how to calculate it) on the graph . (It's the green line on the diagram.)

7) The **break-even point** is where the **revenue** line crosses the **total costs** line.

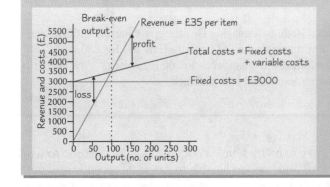

Changing either the **variable costs** or the **price** of the products will affect the break-even point.

This graph shows that if Harry **increased the price** of the T-shirts to £35 each, his break-even output would be **lowered** to 100 units. You could also work this out using the formula for break-even output:

Contribution per unit = £35 – £5 = **£30**
Break-even output = £3000 ÷ £30 = **100**

Break-Even Analysis

The *Margin of Safety* is the amount between *Current Output* and *Break Even*

Margin of safety = current output – break-even output

1) OK, back to Harry's T-shirt business again. The diagram on the right shows the margin of safety for Harry's business when his output is 250 T-shirts. If Harry sells **250** T-shirts, the margin of safety is 250 – 150 = **100** — he could sell up to 100 fewer T-shirts before he started losing money.

2) If his output changed to **300** T-shirts, the margin of safety would go up to 300 – 150 = **150**.

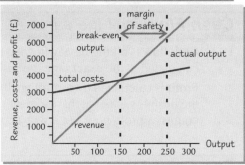

3) Knowing the break-even point and margin of safety allows businesses to make **important decisions** — if Harry's calculations show that his T-shirt business has a low margin of safety, he can take action to increase it by either **lowering his costs** or **increasing his revenue**.

4) This would **lower** his break-even point, so he'd have a **greater** margin of safety. A big margin of safety is useful for a business because it means less risk.

Break-Even Analysis has *Advantages* and *Disadvantages*

<u>Advantages of break-even analysis</u>	<u>Disadvantages of break-even analysis</u>
It's **easy** to do. If you can plot figures on a graph accurately, you can do break-even analysis.	Break-even analysis assumes that **variable costs** always rise steadily. This isn't always the case — a business can get **discounts** for buying in bulk so costs don't go up in **direct proportion** to output.
It's **quick** — managers can see the **break-even point** and **margin of safety** immediately so they can take **quick action** to cut costs or increase sales if they need to **increase** their margin of safety.	Break-even analysis is simple for a **single product** — but most businesses sell lots of different products, so looking at the business as a whole can get a lot more complicated.
Break-even charts let businesses **forecast** how variations in sales will affect **costs**, **revenue** and **profits** and, most importantly, how variations in **price** and **costs** will affect how **much** they **need** to **sell**.	If the **data** is wrong, then the **results** will be wrong.
Businesses can use break-even analysis to help **persuade** the bank to give them a **loan**.	Break-even analysis assumes the business sells **all the products**, without any wastage. But, for example, a restaurant business will end up throwing away food if fewer customers turn up than they're expecting.
Break-even analysis influences decisions on whether **new products** are launched or not — if the business would need to sell an unrealistic volume of products to break even, they would probably decide **not** to launch the product.	Break-even analysis only tells you how many units you **need** to sell to break even. It doesn't tell you how many you're **actually going to sell**.

Practice Questions

Q1 Write down the formula for contribution, and the formula for break-even output.

Q2 Write down two advantages and two disadvantages of break-even analysis.

Answer on p.77.

Exam Questions

Q1 Bob is deciding whether to set up in business selling fishing equipment. Evaluate the value of break-even analysis in helping Bob decide whether or not to go ahead with the business. (10 marks)

Q2 Muneer Khan has a small restaurant. The average price per customer per meal is £13. The variable costs of materials and labour per meal are £5. The fixed costs of the restaurant are £1000 per month. Calculate the break-even number of customers per month. (4 marks)

Ah, give us a break...

You might be asked to calculate the break-even point or draw it on a graph, so make sure you can do both. Make sure you can also give examples of how the break-even point is used by businesses to make decisions, and learn some advantages and disadvantages of break-even analysis. Then give yourself a pat on the back and move on to the next page. Yippee...

Cash Flow Forecasting

Cash flow is money flowing in and out of a business. It's vital to have enough money to meet your immediate debts — otherwise the people you owe money to start getting very cross.

Cash Flow isn't the same as Profit

1) **Cash flow** is all the money flowing **into** and **out of** the business over a period of time, calculated at the **exact time** the cash **enters** or **leaves** the bank account or till.

2) **Profit** is calculated by recording all transactions that will **lead** to cash going **in** or **out** of the business either at that moment or at some point in the **future**. Selling something on credit counts as profit now, but it won't count as cash flow until the customer actually pays for it.

The Cash Flow Cycle is the Gap between Money Going Out and Coming In

1) Businesses need to **pay money out** for fixed assets (e.g. buildings, machinery and vehicles) and operating costs to fulfil an order **before** they **get paid** for that order. The money needed to run a business from day to day is called **working capital**. New firms **need money** to spend on start-up costs **before** they've made any sales at all.

2) This **delay** between money going out and money coming in is the **cash flow cycle**.

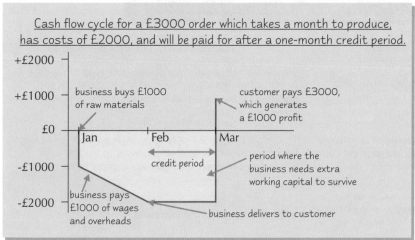

Cash flow cycle for a £3000 order which takes a month to produce, has costs of £2000, and will be paid for after a one-month credit period.

> \ \ \ \ | | / / /
> Bankruptcy is for sole
> traders/partnerships,
> and insolvency is
> for companies.
> / / / | | \ \ \ \

3) It's important to make sure there's always **enough money** available to pay **suppliers** and **wages**. Not paying suppliers and employees can be something of a **disaster**.

4) If a business **produces too much**, they'll have to **pay** suppliers and staff **so much** that they'll go **bankrupt** or **insolvent** before they have the chance to **get paid** by their customers. This is called **overtrading**.

Cash flow calculations are pretty much **the most important thing** to a business in the **short term**. Businesses need cash to survive. Looking at the **long term**, **profit** is important — making profit is the main objective for businesses.

Businesses have Various Canny Tricks to Improve cash flow

1) Businesses try to **reduce the time** between **paying** suppliers and **getting money** from customers. They try to get their **suppliers** to give them a **longer** credit period — and give their **customers** a **shorter** credit period. It's important to **balance** the need to manage cash flow with the need to keep suppliers and customers **happy** — you don't want customers to go elsewhere.

2) Businesses can try to hold less **stock**, so less cash is tied up in stock.

3) **Credit controllers** keep **debtors** in control. They set credit limits and remind debtors to pay up.

4) **Debt factoring** gives instant cash to businesses whose customers haven't paid their invoices. Banks and other financial institutions act as **debt factoring agents**. The agent pays the business about **80%** of the value of the invoice as an **instant cash advance**. The agent gets the customer to pay up, and then **keeps** about **5%** of the value of the invoice — debt factoring costs money and the agent needs to make a living.

5) **Sale and leaseback** is when businesses **sell** equipment to **raise capital**, and then **lease** (rent) the equipment back. That way, they get a big **lump sum** from the sale, and pay a **little** bit of money each month for the lease of the equipment. Of course, they don't get to own the equipment again unless they get enough cash to buy it back — and they have to pay the lease in the meantime.

Cash Flow Forecasting

Businesses make Cash Flow Forecasts to help them make decisions

1) **Cash flow forecasts** (also called cash budgets) show the amount of money that managers **expect** to **come into** the business and **flow out** of the business over a period of time in the **future**.

2) Managers can use cash flow forecasts to **make sure** they always have **enough** cash around to pay **suppliers** and **employees**. They can **predict** when they'll be **short of cash**, and arrange a **loan** or **overdraft** in time.

3) Businesses show cash flow forecasts to **banks** and venture capitalists when trying to get **loans** and other finance. Cash flow forecasts prove that the business has an idea of where it's going to be in the future.

4) **Established** firms base forecasts on **past experience**. **New** firms have no past data, so their forecast should consider the business' **capacity**, experiences of **similar firms** and customer behaviour trends shown by **market research**.

Here's how to Construct and Interpret a Cash Flow Forecast

Example: A new firm starts up with a loan of £18 000 and £5000 of capital. It expects to sell £5000 of goods in January, £35 000 in February, £35 000 in March and £40 000 in April. All customers will get a **one month credit period**. Wages and rent will cost £15 000 each month, and other costs are expected to be £5000 in January, £8000 in February, £2000 in March and £2000 in April.

This shows cash coming in from <u>sales</u> and from the initial <u>start-up loan</u>.

This shows <u>cash going out</u> to pay for the firm's <u>costs</u>.

<u>Net cash flow = total cash in – total costs</u>

The <u>opening balance</u> is money in the bank at the start, in this case £5000.

	Item	Jan	Feb	Mar	Apr
Cash in	Sales revenue		£5000	£35000	£35000
	Other cash in	£18000			
	Total cash in	**£18000**	**£5000**	**£35000**	**£35000**
Cash out	Wages and rent	£15000	£15000	£15000	£15000
	Advertising/other costs	£5000	£8000	£2000	£2000
	Total costs	**£20000**	**£23000**	**£17000**	**£17000**
Net monthly cash flow	Net cash flow	(£2000)	(£18000)	£18000	£18000
	Opening balance	£5000	£3000	(£15000)	£3000
	Closing balance	**£3000**	**(£15000)**	**£3000**	**£21000**

April's sales revenue isn't included because it won't be paid until May, by the way.

Figures in brackets are <u>negative</u>.

According to this, the business will have £21 000 in the bank by the end of April. <u>But</u> it'll still owe £18 000 from the start-up loan ...

<u>Closing balance = opening balance + net cash flow</u>

The <u>closing</u> balance for <u>last month</u> is <u>this month's opening balance</u>.

In the exam, they might ask you to fill in missing figures in a cash flow forecast, amend (change) it, draw a new one from scratch, or analyse it to say what financial position the business is likely to be in in the future.

Cash Flow Forecasting isn't always accurate

1) Cash flow forecasts can be based on **false assumptions** about what's going to happen.

2) Circumstances can **change suddenly** after the forecast's been made. **Costs** can **go up**. Machinery can **break down** and need mending. **Competitors** can put their prices up or down, which **affects sales**.

3) Good cash flow forecasting needs lots of **experience** and lots of **research** into the market.

4) A **false forecast** can have **disastrous** results. A business that runs out of cash can go **bankrupt** or **insolvent**.

Practice Questions

Q1 What's the difference between profit and cash flow?

Q2 Give two reasons why a cash flow forecast is useful to someone setting up their own small business.

Q3 If a company has total cash in of £8000 and total costs of £9500, what is its net cash flow?

Q4 If a company has an opening balance of £20 000 and its net cash flow is (£7000), what is the closing balance?

Q5 How can you work out a company's opening balance in any given month?

Answers on p.77.

Exam Questions

Q1 Examine the ways in which a business can improve its cash flow. (9 marks)

Q2 To what extent can a business successfully and accurately predict future cash flow? Explain your answer. (12 marks)

Dunno 'bout you, but cash flows through my wallet like water...

Cash flow is vitally important — without it, businesses can go bankrupt or insolvent. Make sure you know how to calculate the figures in the table on this page. It can be slightly tricky to start with, so go over it a few times until you really get it. Don't forget to learn the ways that businesses can improve their cash flow too. It's tricky but it'll be worth it in the exam.

Setting Budgets

Businesses make financial plans. They set targets for how much money they're going to make, and how much they're going to spend. Then they check to see how they've done. It sounds simple enough...

Questions about budgets in the exam will ask you to fill in missing figures or amend (change) a budget.

A **Budget** is a **Financial Plan** for the future

A **budget** forecasts **future earnings** and **future spending**, usually over a 12 month period. Businesses use different budgets to estimate different things. There are three types of budget:

1) **Income budgets** forecast the amount of money that will come into the company as revenue. In order to do this, the company needs to predict **how much** it will sell, and at what **price**. Managers estimate this using their **sales figures** from previous years, as well as **market research.**

2) **Expenditure budgets** predict what the business' **total costs** will be for the year, taking into account both fixed and variable costs. Since variable costs increase with output, managers need to predict what the output will be (based on how much they expect to sell).

3) The **profit budget** uses the totals from the income and expenditure budgets to calculate what the expected **profit** (or **loss**) will be for that year.

Budgets affect **All Areas** of the business

1) The expenditure budget forecasts **total** expenditure. This is broken down into **department** expenditure budgets — each department is allotted a certain amount of money to spend.

2) Department expenditure budgets are broken down into budgets for **specific activities** within the department.

3) **Budget holders** are people **responsible** for spending or generating the money for each budget. For example, the budget holder of the expenditure budget for marketing would be the head of the marketing department.

4) The **master budgets** help businesses understand their cash flow situation **as a whole**, and the department and activity budgets help local managers control and coordinate their work.

5) Budgets **set targets** that can be used to **control** or **motivate** staff, depending on management style.

The **Budget Setting** process involves **Research** and **Negotiation**

1) To set the **income budget**, businesses **research** and **predict** how sales are going to go up and down through the year, so that they can make a good prediction of **sales revenue**.

2) To set the **expenditure budget** for **production**, businesses research how labour costs, raw materials costs, taxes and inflation are going to go up over the year. They can then figure out the **costs** of producing the volume of product that they think they're going to sell.

3) Annual budgets are usually agreed by **negotiation** — when budget holders have a say in setting their budgets, they're **motivated** to achieve them.

4) Budgets should **stretch** the abilities of the business, but they must be **achievable**. **Unrealistically** high income budgets or low expenditure budgets will **demotivate** staff. No one likes being asked to do the **impossible**.

5) Once they've agreed the budget, budget holders **keep checking** performance against the budget. This is called **variance analysis**. There's more about variance and variance analysis on p. 34-35.

Budgets have **Advantages** and **Disadvantages**

Benefits of budgeting	Drawbacks of budgeting
• Budgets help **control** income and expenditure. They show where the money goes.	• Budgeting can cause **resentment** and rivalry if departments have to compete for money.
• Budgeting forces managers to **review** their activities.	• Budgets can be **restrictive**. Fixed budgets stop firms responding to changing market conditions.
• Budgets let heads of department **delegate** authority to budget holders. Getting authority is **motivating**.	• Budgeting is **time-consuming**. Managers can get too preoccupied with setting and reviewing budgets, and forget to focus on the real issues of **winning business** and **understanding** the **customer**.
• Budgets allow departments to **coordinate** spending.	
• Budgets help managers either **control** or **motivate** staff. Meeting a budget target is **satisfying**.	

Setting Budgets

Budgets can be *Updated Every Year* or developed from *Scratch*

1) **Start-up businesses** have to develop their budgets **from scratch** (known as **zero budgeting**). This is difficult to do because they don't have much information to base their decisions on — they can't take into account the previous year's sales or expenditure. This means that their budgets are likely to be **inaccurate**.

2) After the first year, a business must decide whether to follow the **historical budgeting** method, or to continue using the **zero budgeting** method.

Historical budgets are updated each year

1) This year's budget is based on a percentage increase or decrease from last year's budget. For example, a business expecting 10% revenue growth might add 10% to the advertising, wages and raw materials purchasing budgets.

2) Historical budgeting is **quick** and **simple**, but it assumes that business conditions stay **unchanged** each year. This isn't always the case — for instance, a product at the introduction stage of its **life cycle** (see p.62) needs more money spent on advertising than one in the growth or maturity stages.

Zero budgeting means starting from scratch each year

1) Budget holders **start** with a budget of **£0**, and have to **get approval** to spend money on activities.

2) They have to **plan** all the year's activities, ask for money to spend on them, and be prepared to **justify** their requests to the finance director. Budget holders need good **negotiating** skills for this.

3) Zero budgeting takes much **longer** to complete than historical budgets.

4) If zero budgeting is done properly it's **more accurate** than historical budgeting.

Budgets affect how *Flexible* a business can be

1) **Fixed budgets** provide **discipline** and **certainty**. This is especially important fora business with **liquidity** problems — fixed budgets help control **cash flow**.

2) **Fixed budgeting** means budget holders have to stick to their budget plans throughout the year — even if market conditions change. This can **prevent** a firm reacting to **new opportunities** or **threats** that they didn't know about when they set the budget.

3) **Flexible budgeting** allows budgets to be altered in response to significant changes in the market or economy.

Mary Lou had no problems with flexibility

4) **Zero budgeting** gives a business more **flexibility** than **historical budgeting**.

Practice Questions

Q1 Name the three main types of budget that a business will set, stating what each tells you.

Q2 If a business has an income budget of £125 000 and a profit budget of £30 000, what is its expenditure budget?

Q3 State three benefits and three drawbacks of using budgets.

Q4 What is historical budgeting?

Q5 Explain the difference between fixed and flexible budgets.

Answer on p. 77.

Exam Questions

Q1 To what extent might fixed budgets help a manufacturer in the fast-changing computer software sector? (15 marks)

Q2 (a) Discuss the benefits that setting a budget will have for a new business. (6 marks)
(b) Discuss the problems that a new business might have in setting budgets for the first time. (9 marks)

I set myself a word budget today and I'm just about to run out...

Budgets are multi-purpose — they help businesses forecast their future spending, and they can help to motivate people, too. Luckily, you won't get marked on how good you are at budgeting in the exam — the examiners are only interested in how well you understand income, expenditure and profit budgets, why businesses use them, and how they set them.

Variances

Variance is the difference between actual and budgeted spend. Understanding variances helps managers control business performance, and it'll help you sail through your exams too, with a bit of luck.

Variance is the Difference between Actual figures and Budget figures

1) A variance means the business is performing either **worse** or **better** than expected.

2) A **favourable variance** leads to **increased profit**. If revenue's more than the budget says it's going to be, that's a favourable variance. If costs are below the cost predictions in the budget, that's a favourable variance.

3) An **adverse variance** is a difference that **reduces profits**. **Selling fewer items** than the income budget predicts or **spending more** on an advert than the expenditure budget for marketing allows is an adverse variance.

4) If £10 000 is spent on raw materials in a month when the budget was only £6000, the variance is £6000 − £10000 = −£4000, so there is a £4000 **adverse variance.**

5) Variances **add up**. For example, if actual sales exceed budgeted sales by £3000 and expenditure on raw materials is £2000 below budget, the variance is £3000 + £2000 = £5000, so there's a combined **favourable variance** of £5000. This is called **cumulative variance**.

6) Variances can be calculated for each budget each month, for each budget as a running total, and for groups of budgets as a monthly or running total variance:

(A) means an adverse variance.
(F) means a favourable variance.

	Jan Budget	Jan Actual	Jan Variance	Feb Budget	Feb Actual	Feb Variance	Cumulative Variance
Revenue	£100k	£90k	£10k (A)	£110k	£110k	£0	£10k (A)
Wages	£40k	£30k	£10k (F)	£40k	£41k	£1k (A)	£9k (F)
Rent	£10k	£10k	£0	£10k	£11k	£1k (A)	£1k (A)
Other costs	£5k	£6k	£1k (A)	£5k	£6k	£1k (A)	£2k (A)
Total costs	£55k	£46k	£9k (F)	£55k	£58k	£3k (A)	£6k (F)

Variances can be Bad — even when they say you're doing Better than Expected

1) When variances occur, it means that what has happened is **not** what the business was expecting. Businesses need to **know** about variances so that they can find out **why** they have occurred.

2) It's extremely important to spot **adverse** variances as **soon** as possible. It's important to find out which budget holder is responsible — and to take action to fix the problem.

3) It's **also** important to **investigate favourable variances**. Favourable variances may mean that the budget targets weren't **stretching** enough — so the business needs to set more **difficult targets**. The business also needs to understand **why** the performance is better than expected — if one department is **doing something right**, the business can **spread** this throughout the organisation.

Variances are caused by several factors — Internal and External

External Factors Cause Variance

1) **Competitor behaviour** and changing **fashions** may increase or reduce **demand** for products.

2) Changes in the **economy** can change how much workers' wages cost the business.

3) The cost of **raw materials** can go up — e.g. if a harvest fails.

Internal Factors Cause Variance

1) Improving **efficiency** (e.g. by introducing automated production equipment) causes **favourable** variances.

2) A business might **overestimate** the amount of money it can save by streamlining its production methods.

3) A business might **underestimate** the **cost** of making a change to its organisation.

4) Changing the selling price changes sales revenue — this creates variance if it happens after the budget's been set.

5) Internal causes of variance are a **serious concern**. They suggest that internal **communication** needs improvement.

Variances

Variance Analysis means Identifying and Explaining variances

1) Variance analysis means **spotting** variances and figuring out **why** they've happened, so that action can be taken to fix them.

2) **Small** variances aren't a big problem. They can actually help to **motivate** employees. Staff try to **catch up** and sort out small **adverse** variances themselves. Small **favourable** variances can motivate staff to **keep on** doing whatever they were doing to create a favourable variance.

3) **Large** variances can **demotivate**. Staff don't work hard if there are large favourable variances — they **don't see the need**. Staff can get demotivated by a large **adverse** variance — they may feel that the task is **impossible**, or that they've **already failed**.

Businesses have to Do Something about variances

When variances occur, businesses can either change what the **business** is doing to make it fit the budget, or change the **budget** to make it fit what the **business** is doing. There are three factors that they need take into account to make this decision:

1) Businesses need to **beware** of chopping and changing the budget **too much**.

2) Changing the budget **removes certainty** — which removes one of the big benefits of budgets.

3) Altering budgets can also make them **less motivating** — when staff start to expect that management will change targets instead of doing something to change performance, they don't see the point in trying any more.

Businesses Try to Fix Adverse Variances

1) They can change the **marketing mix**. **Cutting prices** will increase sales — but only if the demand is price elastic (see p.68). **Updating** the product might make it more attractive to customers. Businesses can also look for a **new market** for the product, or change the **promotional strategy** — e.g. by advertising the product more or doing point of sales promotion.

2) **Streamlining production** makes the business more **efficient**, so this reduces costs.

3) They can try to motivate **employees** to **work harder**.

4) Businesses can try to cut costs by asking their **suppliers** for a **better deal**.

Businesses Try to Fix Favourable Variances

1) If the favourable variance is caused by a **pessimistic** budget, they set more **ambitious targets** next time.

2) If the variance is because of **increased productivity** in one part of the business, they try to get everyone else doing whatever was **responsible** for the improvement, and set higher targets in the next budget.

Practice Questions

Q1 Define variance.

Q2 If a business sets an expenditure budget of £15 000 for marketing, and the actual expenditure for marketing is £18 000, how much is the variance and what type of variance is it?

Q3 Why are variances a concern for businesses?

Q4 State two external factors and two internal factors that cause variance.

Q5 How do businesses deal with variances?

Exam Question

Q1 (a) Using the figures in the table on p.34, calculate monthly and cumulative variances for March. Assume all budgets remain the same as February, and that actual sales are £120k, wages are £39k, rent is £11k and other costs are £5k. (10 marks)

(b) Explain what your answer to (a) suggests about the budget planning process for this company. (6 marks)

Answers on p.77.

Variance is one of those words that looks odd if you stare at it enough...

Variance variance variance variance variance... ahem... anyway. As well as knowing what businesses do when they set a budget, you need to know what they do when the real-life results don't quite match up to what the budget says. They don't panic and run about shouting "beeble beeble" in the car park. They just sort it out so it doesn't happen next time.

Measuring and Increasing Profit

Businesses need to measure their profit to find out how successful (or unsuccessful) they are.

Profit is Not the same as Revenue

1) **Revenue** is the amount of money that a business receives from sales of its products (see p. 26). But they **don't keep** all of it — the business also has **costs**.

2) When the **costs** are **deducted** from its **revenue**, what is left is the **profit**.

3) If the business' **costs** are **greater** than its **revenue**, it will make a **loss** instead of a profit.

Businesses want to Increase their profits

1) Most businesses exist to make a **profit** — if a business makes large profits then it is **successful**. Even successful businesses want to **increase profits** and become **more successful**.

2) Businesses can **improve** their **profits** by increasing their **prices** (if the demand for their products is price inelastic — see p. 68) or **reducing** their prices to increase **demand** (if demand is price elastic). They could also try to reduce their **costs**, or use **marketing** to increase demand so that they sell more and make bigger profits.

3) Businesses **measure** their profits on a regular basis. They **compare** their profits from the current period (usually a year) to the profits from previous periods to measure their **progress**.

4) If profits go **down**, this is **bad news**, even if the business is still making large profits. For example, if a business makes a profit of £100 million in a year, this might sound like good news, but if the previous year's profits were £125 million then it's a **bad sign**.

5) This is why businesses work out the **percentage increase** or **decrease** in their profits from year to year — it makes it easy to see how well they're performing in comparison with other years.

6) If profits are decreasing, the business needs to investigate **why** this is happening and **take action** to resolve the problem.

> *In the exam, set your workings out like the formula.*

The formula for measuring the **percentage change** in profit is:

$$\text{Percentage Change in Profit} = \frac{\text{Current Year's Profit} - \text{Previous Year's Profit}}{\text{Previous Year's Profit}} \times 100\%$$

If a business makes a profit of **£20 000** in one year and **£30 000** the next year, the percentage change in profit is (£30 000 – £20 000) ÷ £20 000 × 100% = 50% — a **50% rise** in profits.

If a business makes a profit of **£10 000** in a year after having made a profit of **£15 000** in the previous year, the percentage change in profit is (£10 000 – £15 000) ÷ £15 000 × 100% = –33% — a **fall** in profits of **33%**.

There are Two Types of profit — Gross Profit and Net Profit

1) **Gross profit** is the amount left over when the **cost of making the products** is taken away. You can calculate **gross profit** by subtracting **variable costs** from the **revenue**.

> **Gross Profit = Revenue – Variable Costs**

2) **Net profit** takes into consideration not only the cost of actually producing each product, but also the **fixed costs** involved in running the business (for more on fixed and variable costs, see p. 26). You get the **net profit** by subtracting both **fixed costs** and **variable costs** from the **revenue**.

> **Net Profit = Revenue – (Fixed Costs + Variable Costs)**

Polly hoped that her net profit would increase enough for her to be able to make a whole dress.

Example

Hannah's Hammers is a small company selling hammers with a floral design. The variable cost of producing each hammer is **£2**, and they are sold for **£5** each. Hannah also has fixed costs of **£15 000** a year.

If Hannah sells **10 000** hammers in a year, her **revenue** is 10 000 × £5 = **£50 000**.

Hannah's **gross profit** is £50 000 – (2 × 10 000) = **£30 000**.

Her **net profit** is £50 000 – (£15 000 + £20 000) = **£15 000**.

Measuring and Increasing Profit

Net Profit Margins show how Profitable a business or product is

1) ·Net profit margins measure the relationship between the **net profits made** and the **volume of sales**. They tell you what **percentage** of the selling price of a product is actually **net profit**.

2) Businesses can calculate their profit margins for **individual products**, or for the company **as a whole**.

3) The net profit margin is expressed as a percentage — the formula is:

$$\text{Net Profit Margin} = \frac{\text{Net Profit}}{\text{Revenue}} \times 100\%$$

4) It's best to have a **high** net profit margin, although it does depend on the type of business.

5) The net profit margin can be improved by **raising prices** or **lowering the cost of making the products** or (most importantly) the **fixed costs**. Raising prices might cause **demand** to **fall** though (see price elasticity of demand, p. 68), so **increasing** the net profit **margin** too much could end up having a **negative** effect on **profits**. Similarly, **reducing** the **cost** of making the products could be **risky** if it affects the level of **quality**.

6) A business can improve its overall net profit margin by **stopping** selling products with a **low net profit margin**.

7) If a business has a revenue of £60 000 and a net profit of £18 000, its net profit margin is: (£18 000 ÷ £60 000) × 100% = **30%**.

8) If the business manages to reduce its fixed costs the following year by £3000, and turnover stays the same, the new net profit will be £21 000, so the net profit margin will rise to (£21 000 ÷ £60 000) × 100% = **35%**

Return on Capital Employed (ROCE) is an Important Profitability Ratio

1) The **return on capital employed** (ROCE) is considered to be the **best** way of analysing **profitability**.

2) The **ROCE** tells you how much money is **made** by the business, compared to how much money's been **put into** the business. It tells you how good the business is at generating profits from money invested.

3) In order to calculate the ROCE, you need to know what the **net profit** is, **excluding** any profit made from **one-off activities** (e.g. if a business raises £700 by putting on a raffle, this **shouldn't** be included in the ROCE calculation).

4) You also need to know the figure for **capital employed**. Capital employed means all the money that has been **invested** in the business, so it refers to the money that has come into the business from **loans** and **shares**.

5) ROCE is expressed as a percentage — the formula for calculating it is:

$$\text{Return on Capital Employed} = \frac{\text{Net Profit}}{\text{Capital Employed}} \times 100\%$$

6) A good **ROCE** is about **20%**, but 10-15% is OK. It's important to compare the ROCE with the Bank of England interest rate at the time — if the return is less than the interest rate then the investors would have been better off putting their money in the bank.

7) A business can improve its ROCE by using part of its net profit to **pay off some debts** — this will reduce capital employed. Another way to improve the ROCE is by making the business more **efficient** to **increase net profit**.

Practice Questions

Answer on p. 78.

Q1 If a business makes a profit of £50 000 in 2006 and £52 000 in 2007, what is the percentage change in profit?

Q2 What is the formula for calculating Return on Capital Employed?

Q3 Give two ways in which Return on Capital Employed can be improved.

Exam Questions

Q1 Calculate the ROCE for a business with a net profit of £100 000 and capital employed of £40 000. (2 marks)

Answers on p. 78.

Q2 A business has a revenue of £2 million. Its gross profit is £750 000, and its fixed costs are £250 000.
(a) Calculate the net profit margin. (4 marks)
(b) Recommend what the business could do to improve the net profit margin. Explain why you're making this recommendation. (6 marks)

I'm just about 100% fed up with all these percentage calculations...

OK, I admit this hasn't been the world's most interesting page but this is all really important stuff, so make sure you get your head around it before moving on. You need to be able to calculate net profit margin and ROCE, so learn the formulas — you also need to understand what they actually mean for a business, and how businesses can improve their profitability.

Business Structures

The structure of a business depends on its size, its geographical distribution, the kind of product or service it offers, and the history and culture of the organisation.

Structure and Hierarchy are shown by an Organisational Chart

1) The traditional business structure is a series of levels, where each level has responsibility for, and authority over, the levels below. This is called a **hierarchy**.

2) An **organisational chart** sets out who has **authority** to make decisions, and who has **responsibility** for making them.

3) It shows who individual employees are **accountable** to — who is directly **above** them in the hierarchy.

4) It shows who employees are **responsible** for — who is directly **below** them in the hierarchy.

5) The chart also shows how the organisation is divided up. This chart is divided by **function**, e.g. into a production department, a marketing department etc., or it can be divided by **product** or **geographical area**.

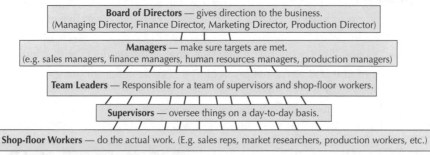

Board of Directors — gives direction to the business.
(Managing Director, Finance Director, Marketing Director, Production Director)

Managers — make sure targets are met.
(e.g. sales managers, finance managers, human resources managers, production managers)

Team Leaders — Responsible for a team of supervisors and shop-floor workers.

Supervisors — oversee things on a day-to-day basis.

Shop-floor Workers — do the actual work. (E.g. sales reps, market researchers, production workers, etc.)

Structures can be "Tall" or "Flat"

1) Organisations with **lots of levels** in their hierarchy are called "**tall**". They have a large number of people between the top and the bottom. Tall structures have a long **chain of command**. The chain of command is the path of **communication** and **authority** up and down the hierarchy.

2) If the structure is **too tall**, it affects **communication**. Messages take a **long time** to get from one end of the chain of command to the other, and they can get **garbled** on the way. **Decisions** take a long time to make, and there's a lot of **paperwork** to deal with.

3) "**Flat**" organisations only have a few levels in the hierarchy. People may be given more responsibility and freedom.

4) If the structure is **too flat**, then managers can get **overwhelmed** by too many people reporting to them.

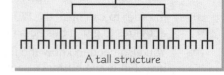

A tall structure

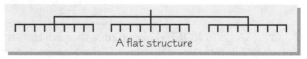

A flat structure

Structures can have broad or narrow Spans of Control

1) The **span of control** is the **number of people** who report directly to a manager. Managers in **flat** organisational structures have **wide** spans of control. This means they have a lot of workers answering to them.

2) Managers in tall structures have **narrower** spans of control — they aren't responsible for as many people. This allows them to **monitor** the people who report to them **more closely**.

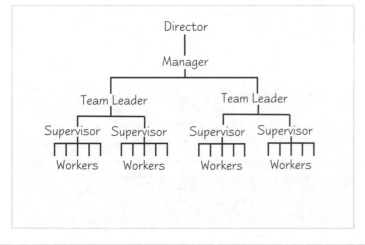

3) If the span of control is **too broad**, managers can find it hard to manage **effectively**.

4) If the span of control is **too narrow**, workers can become **demotivated** — they may feel that they're being **micromanaged** (over-managed) by interfering bosses.

5) **Traditionally**, business experts thought it would be hard for a manager to keep a close eye on workers if the span of control was bigger than about 6 people. But if the workers are all doing the **same routine task**, they don't need as much close supervision — so a span of control of 10-12 people (or more) is fine.

Business Structures

Centralised Structures keep Authority for decisions at the Top

In an organisation where decision-making is **centralised**, all decisions are made by **one person**, or one committee of **senior managers** right at the **top** of the business.

Advantages of Centralisation	Disadvantages of Centralisation
Business leaders tend to have plenty of **experience**.	Not many people are **expert** enough in **all aspects** of the business.
Managers get an **overview** of the whole business.	Excluding employees from decision-making can be **demotivating**.
Senior managers understand **central** budgeting restrictions and can make decisions to save the **whole business** money.	Decisions can take a **long time**. The organisation reacts **slowly** to change, and can end up a couple of steps behind its competitors.

Decentralised Structures share out the Authority to make decisions

1) Decentralisation **shares out authority** to more **junior** employees.

2) Giving responsibility for decision-making to people below you is called **delegation**.

3) **National** and **multinational** organisations **decentralise** decision-making and delegate power to **regional** managers.

Advantages of Decentralisation	Disadvantages of Decentralisation
Involvement in decision-making **motivates** employees.	Subordinates may not have enough **experience** to make decisions.
Employees can use **expert knowledge** of their sector.	**Inconsistencies** may develop between sectors in a business.
Decisions can be made more **quickly** without having to ask senior managers.	Junior employees may not be able to see the **overall situation** and **needs** of an organisation.

Delayering removes layers of hierarchy

Delayering is a key way in which a manager can **alter** the **structure** of a business. Changing the structure of the business can improve **performance** and increase **competitiveness**.

1) Delayering is when a business **removes** a layer of the hierarchy from its organisational structure — usually a layer of managers from somewhere in the **middle** of the hierarchy.

2) Delayering helps to **lower costs**. Cutting management jobs can save a lot of money in salaries.

3) After delayering, you get a **flatter** structure with **broader** spans of control. It's worth being careful not to **overdo** it. If a company is delayered to too great an extent, managers can end up **stressed** and overworked with **huge, vast-reaching** spans of control.

Zoë didn't hold back her feelings towards the company's plans to delayer.

4) Delayering can give junior employees **enhanced roles** with more responsibility.

5) Some businesses use delayering as an **excuse** to cut jobs.

Practice Questions

Q1 Why might a flat structure be popular with junior employees in a business?

Q2 What is meant by "span of control"?

Q3 Give two advantages of a centralised decision-making structure.

Q4 Give two disadvantages of a decentralised decision-making structure.

Exam Questions

Q1 A firm of management consultants have advised Douglas McLeod to delayer and flatten the structure of his business.
(a) What is meant by flattening the structure of the business? (2 marks)
(b) Discuss the factors that Douglas should think about before starting to delayer. (10 marks)

Q2 To what extent is a wide span of control desirable for a manager in a business? (10 marks)

Delayering — isn't that taking off your cardigan when it's warm...

Delayering can be a great way of simplifying things and saving money — if your middle managers are useless David Brent types, getting rid of them is the kindest thing to do, really. Both tall and flat structures have pros and cons — learn them in case you get asked to evaluate a particular kind of business structure, or in case you bump into an architect at a party...

Measuring Workforce Effectiveness

A business needs to measure the effectiveness of every resource used, and that includes its employees.
People don't always like the idea of having their performance measured, but it's good for the business.

Human Resource Management (HRM) keeps the Workforce Flexible

Businesses need to be **flexible** enough to react in a competitive and changing environment. Change comes from consumer **demand**, new **technology** and new **laws**. **Competitors** are constantly joining and leaving the market. A flexible workforce tends to be an effective one, so HRM makes sure that the workforce is **adaptable** to these changes.

1) The main function of Human Resources is to ensure that the business has the **right number of employees** and that they're of the **right quality** in terms of **qualifications and skills**.

2) HRM plans how to **recruit** staff — where to advertise, how to interview, etc.

3) **Human resources strategies** can be **short-term** (e.g. recruiting part-time staff for Christmas sales in retailing) or **long-term** (e.g. anticipating growth or a change in production techniques).

4) Human resources departments also decide how to treat staff while they're working for the business — how to **use their skills**, how to **keep** them working for the company, how to **train** and **reward** them, and eventually how to **terminate** their employment.

5) The HRM department might also set up a **performance management system** to check that human resources are always being used to maximum efficiency. This system calculates performance based on **labour productivity**, **absenteeism**, and **labour turnover**.

Labour Productivity measures How Much each Employee Produces

It's important for companies to know how productive their workforce is, because changes in labour productivity can have a massive impact on the business. This is especially true in **labour-intensive** firms, where labour costs are a high proportion of total costs.

$$\text{Labour Productivity} = \frac{\text{Output per period}}{\text{Number of employees}}$$

Dave's productivity currently stood at 900 rabbits per hour.

The **higher** the labour productivity, the **better** the workforce is performing.
As labour productivity **increases**, labour costs per unit **fall**.

Example: A factory has 30 workers per shift working 3 shifts per day to produce 9000 DVD players per week.
Productivity = 9000 ÷ 90 workers = **100** DVD players per worker per week.

Ways to increase labour productivity

1) Labour productivity can be improved by **improving worker motivation** (see p.44-45).

2) **Training** can make workers more productive.

Businesses need to consider the Consequences of Increasing Productivity

1) Some companies **reward** increased productivity. Paying workers using a **piece rate** system (see p.45) encourages staff to produce more. Managers should take care that **quality** doesn't suffer in the process.

2) Increasing labour productivity means **redundancies** and **job losses** unless sales increase. Businesses need to **plan** for the consequences of improved productivity to avoid upsetting staff.

3) Businesses must **balance** productivity against things like product **quality** and long-term worker **motivation**.

Measuring Workforce Effectiveness

Absenteeism measures the Proportion of Time employees are Off Work

$$\text{Absenteeism} = \frac{\text{Number of staff days lost}}{\text{Number of working days}} \times 100\%$$

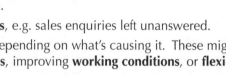

To calculate the number of working days, multiply the number of days that a company operates by its total number of employees and then subtract the number of days holiday it gives its staff.

1) Absenteeism is measured as a percentage. Obviously, **low** is best.

2) You have to analyse figures in the **context** of each industry. For example, **police** officers might have **higher** than average figures because of the dangers and stresses of the job, while **sales** people paid on commission have **lower** rates because they lose pay when off work.

3) **Causes** of absenteeism include poor **working conditions**, poor **relationships** with managers and other staff, **stress** or **disillusionment** with the job, and poor **motivation**.

4) Absenteeism **increases costs**. It results in **lost opportunities**, e.g. sales enquiries left unanswered.

5) There are several ways a firm might **reduce absenteeism**, depending on what's causing it. These might include **job enrichment** (see p.45), improving **working relationships**, improving **working conditions**, or **flexi-time**.

Labour Turnover measures the Proportion of Staff who Leave each year

$$\text{Labour Turnover} = \frac{\text{Number of staff leaving}}{\text{Average number of staff employed}}$$

Work out the part-timers as if they're fractions of a full-time employee. Two people who each work half a week = one person working a whole week.

1) The **higher** the figure, the larger the proportion of workers leaving the firm each year.

2) **External causes** of high labour turnover include changes in regional **unemployment** levels, and the growth of other local firms using staff with **similar skills**.

3) **Internal causes** of high labour turnover include poor motivation of staff, low wages, and a lack of opportunities for promotion. Staff will **join other firms** to increase their pay and job responsibilities.

4) A **poor recruitment** process which selects incompetent candidates will also increase labour turnover.

5) Increased **delegation**, **job enrichment**, higher **wages** and better **training** can reduce employee turnover.

6) Businesses need **some** labour turnover to bring new ideas in. Labour turnover of 0% means no one **ever** leaves.

Benefits of high staff turnover	Disadvantages of high staff turnover
Constant stream of **new ideas** through new staff.	Lack of **loyal** and **experienced** staff who know the business.
Firm can recruit staff who've **already been trained** by competitors — saves money.	Firm **loses** staff it has **trained**, often to direct competitors.
If sales fall, firm can reduce workforce through **natural wastage** rather than costly redundancy.	**Training costs money** and **productivity drops** while new staff get trained.
Enthusiasm of new staff influences other workers.	**Recruitment** costs are high.

Practice Questions

Q1 A company has low labour productivity. Make three suggestions that might help to increase its output.

Q2 A firm operates for 245 days per year. It has 56 full-time staff who get 25 days holiday each. In 2006, holiday aside, staff were absent for a total of 274 staff days. Calculate the firm's absenteeism.

Q3 State two benefits and two drawbacks of a high labour turnover percentage.

Answers on p. 78.

Q4 In 2007, 18 people leave a firm which employs an average of 600 staff. Calculate the firm's labour turnover.

Exam Questions

Q1 Explain why a major employer such as the NHS should be concerned about differing absenteeism percentages in different hospitals, and recommend what action they could take. (10 marks)

Q2 Evaluate potential problems if a firm were to change its production method to improve labour productivity. (6 marks)

I have a flexible workforce — they're always bending the rules...

They're all quite easy really, these equations. Problem is, the numbers alone don't really tell you anything. It's good to have high productivity if you're making something simple, like baked beans, but not necessarily if the product is complicated — a jet plane, for example. The same can't be said for absenteeism though — that's always a bad thing...

Workforce Planning

A good recruitment process means a company has the right number of people with the right skills to do the job.

The **Recruitment Process** can take a long time

There are seven key steps in a successful recruitment process:

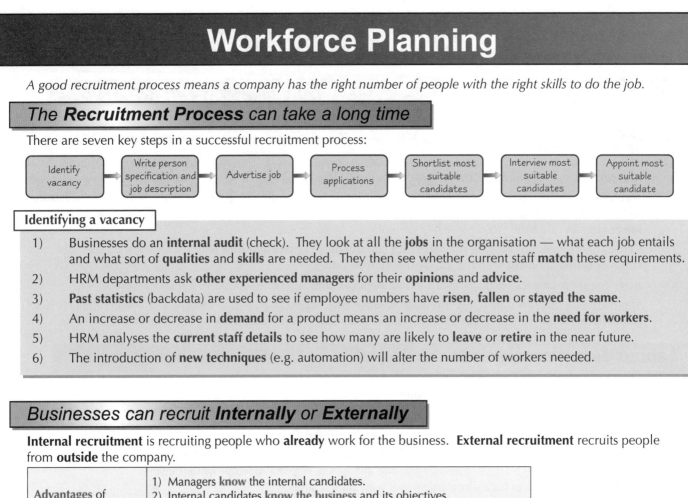

Identify vacancy → Write person specification and job description → Advertise job → Process applications → Shortlist most suitable candidates → Interview most suitable candidates → Appoint most suitable candidate

Identifying a vacancy

1) Businesses do an **internal audit** (check). They look at all the **jobs** in the organisation — what each job entails and what sort of **qualities** and **skills** are needed. They then see whether current staff **match** these requirements.

2) HRM departments ask **other experienced managers** for their **opinions** and **advice**.

3) **Past statistics** (backdata) are used to see if employee numbers have **risen**, **fallen** or **stayed the same**.

4) An increase or decrease in **demand** for a product means an increase or decrease in the **need for workers**.

5) HRM analyses the **current staff details** to see how many are likely to **leave** or **retire** in the near future.

6) The introduction of **new techniques** (e.g. automation) will alter the number of workers needed.

Businesses can recruit **Internally** or **Externally**

Internal recruitment is recruiting people who **already** work for the business. **External recruitment** recruits people from **outside** the company.

Advantages of internal recruitment	1) Managers **know** the internal candidates. 2) Internal candidates **know the business** and its objectives. 3) It's a **shorter** and **less expensive** process than external recruitment. 4) It **motivates** workers by encouraging them to go for promotion.
Disadvantages of internal recruitment	1) Internal promotion leaves **another vacancy** to be filled. 2) It can cause **resentment** among colleagues who aren't selected.
Advantages of external recruitment	1) External recruits bring in **fresh new ideas**. 2) External recruits bring **experience** from other organisations. 3) There's a larger pool of applicants to **choose** from.
Disadvantages of external recruitment	1) Managers **don't know** the applicant. 2) It's usually a **long** and **expensive** process. 3) External recruits usually need a longer **induction** process (see p.43).

External recruitment seemed to have worked for the German police force.

Businesses **advertise** vacancies to external applicants in national and local newspapers, specialist trade magazines, and through employment agencies or job centres. **Where** they advertise the job depends on the **type** of job, the **size** of the organisation and **where** the organisation operates.

Selection — getting the **Right People** for the job

It's obviously important to get the best possible candidate for a job. To have the best chance of getting this, the HR department **analyses** the vacancy and draws up a **job description** and a **person specification**.

1) The **job description** lists the tasks and responsibilities the person appointed will be expected to carry out. It may also state the job title, the location, the nature of the business and other details like salary and conditions (e.g. holiday entitlement, pension arrangements and so on).

2) The **person specification** outlines the ideal profile of the person needed to match the job description. It describes their **qualifications**, experience, interests and **personality**. It's important to know whether the candidate will fit into the **culture** and **atmosphere** of the business, as well as knowing whether they've got a GNVQ in Tourism, or if they can do SQL programming.

3) **Interviews** are the most common way of choosing candidates. Candidates can be interviewed **one-to-one** or by a **panel** of interviewers. Phone interviews are thought to be less effective than **face-to-face** interviews.

4) Some organisations use **assessment centres** to help them **test** candidates. Tests include **psychometric** testing which assesses personality fit, **aptitude** tests which find out how good the candidate is at job tasks, and **group exercises** which show how candidates interact with other people in various situations.

Workforce Planning

Employees need *Training* and *Development*

1) The **first day** or so on the job is usually spent learning the workings of the business, covering the health and safety issues, and meeting key personnel. This is the **induction** part of the human resources cycle.

2) Most new employees need some training — either to learn **new skills** or **improve** and **update** existing skills.

3) Training can be done **off-the-job** — e.g. studying part-time at a local **college**, a short one- or two-day **course** at a business training centre, or **studying at home** for a professional qualification.

On-the-job training can take several forms:

1) The **traditional** way is to sit the new trainee next to an **experienced worker**. The newbie watches and learns from the experienced worker, who is there to answer any questions about the job.

2) **Mentoring** is where the new employee is advised by an experienced worker who acts as **tutor** and guru.

3) **Coaching** gives the trainee **specialised** knowledge and skills, e.g. through **seminars** or **group sessions**. It is often offered **long-term**.

4) **Job rotation** is where the new person **moves around** the organisation and experiences **different jobs**.

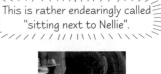

This is rather endearingly called "sitting next to Nellie".

"Lying next to Nellie."

The **Right** kind of *Training* depends on the **Size** and **Type** of business

Advantages of on-the-job training	1) On-the-job training is **easy to organise**. 2) **Costs** of training tend to be **lower**. 3) Training is **specific** to the job in question.
Disadvantages of on-the-job training	1) **Trainer** and **trainee** are **not productive** during training hours. 2) The **trainer** may **not be skilled** in **communication** or may have other **weaknesses**. 3) **Bad** work **practices** can be **passed on** to the trainee. 4) **New ways** of **working** are **not introduced** into the company.

The job that the trainee is employed to do affects the type of training too.

Businesses should **evaluate** their training to see how it's **working**, using clear, measurable objectives. Managers should be able to **compare training costs** with the **financial gains** in overall performance using **cost-benefit analysis**.

Advantages of off-the-job training	1) Off-the-job training uses **specialist trainers**. 2) Training can be more **intensive**. 3) **New theories** and **practices** can be **introduced** to the business. 4) Training occurs **away from** the **distractions** of the job.
Disadvantages of off-the-job training	1) Off-the-job training is more **expensive**. 2) The trainee might **not have access** to **specific tools** used in their job. 3) The trainee is **off-site** and is **not productive**.

Practice Questions

Q1 Outline one advantage and one disadvantage of both internal recruitment and external recruitment.

Q2 Briefly explain the terms "job description" and "person specification".

Q3 Explain the difference between on-the-job training and off-the-job training.

Q4 List and describe three methods of on-the-job training.

Exam Questions

Q1	A major London hotel wants to recruit an experienced accountant. Outline the procedures they may follow in the recruitment process.	(9 marks)
Q2	Evaluate the advantages and disadvantages of internal and external recruitment for a retail organisation with 200 stores nationwide.	(15 marks)

Internal recruitment — sounds painful...

Businesses can use up a lot of time and money on recruitment and training. They're worth doing properly though, because the additional costs tend to pay off in the long run. A well-chosen employee will work harder and stick around for longer (as long as they're being well trained!) so it'll be a while before they have to go through the whole process again. Phew.

Motivating the Workforce

Motivation is important in business — motivated employees get more done than non-motivated employees.
For the past 150 years industrial psychologists and sociologists have tried to figure out what motivates workers...

1) Taylor and Scientific Management — people are in it for the Money

1) In the early 20th century, FW Taylor thought that workers were motivated by **money**.
   He believed workers would do the **minimum** amount of work if left to their own devices.

2) Taylor developed his theories through **work-study** — watching how people work. He did **time and motion studies**, timing work activities with a **stopwatch**. This allowed him to figure out the **most efficient** way to do a job, and then make sure every single worker did it that way. He favoured **division of labour** — breaking work down into a lot of **small repetitive tasks**. This approach is called **scientific management**.

3) Taylor believed in paying workers according to the **quantity** they produced — the most **productive** workers got a **better rate**. He believed that financial incentives would **motivate** workers and raise **productivity**.

4) Scientific management didn't go down well with workers. Increased productivity meant that **fewer workers** were needed — workers worried about losing their jobs.

5) There were other disadvantages, too — increased productivity could lead to a reduction in **quality**. **Supervisors** were needed to monitor efficiency and for quality control purposes.

6) Taylor's approach wouldn't work for modern businesses — it would be seen as **exploitation**. It also ignores the **demotivating** effect of doing very repetitive boring work.

7) However, aspects of Taylor's theory have survived — **piece rate pay** is based on his ideas, and the role of the **supervisor** still exists.

2) Mayo and Human Relations — people are motivated by Social Factors

1) Elton Mayo found that people achieved more when they got **positive attention**. Mayo was doing an experiment on productivity when he found that **all** workers taking part in the experiment became more productive. He worked out that this was because they liked the **social contact** that they got from the experiments, and they liked working in a **group**.

2) Mayo thought management should **pay attention** to workers as individuals, and **involve** them in decision-making. He thought that firms should try to make business goals compatible with workers' goals. This required a **democratic** style of management, as well as lots of **delegation** and good **communication**.

3) He also thought that workers should **socialise** together — outside work as well as at work.

3) Maslow's Hierarchy of Needs — people need Basics first

Maslow said that people start by meeting the needs at the **bottom** of the pyramid. Once they've sorted out those needs, they can move on to the needs on the **next level** up.

Maslow and Herzberg both believed that workers had needs which were specific to them as individuals.

Self-actualisation — meeting potential
Businesses meet these needs by giving the opportunity to develop new skills and take responsibility.

Self-esteem — achievement
Businesses give employees recognition and offer promotion.

Social Needs — friendship, teamwork
Teamworking and social outings are designed to meet these.

Safety — safe work environment with job security
Health and safety policy and secure employment contracts meet these needs.

Basic Physical Needs — food, water, shelter, clothes
Businesses meet these needs by paying workers enough and providing a warm, dry work environment.

The pyramid **looks good** — but it isn't always **obvious** which level an individual is at.

4) Herzberg's Hygiene and Motivating factors — sort out a Good Environment first

In the 1960s, Frederick Herzberg interviewed accountants and engineers to find out what motivated and satisfied them at work. He identified two groups of factors which influenced the motivation of workers:

1) **Hygiene factors** are things like good **company policy**, **supervision**, **working conditions**, **pay**, and **relations** with fellow employees. They don't motivate as such, but if they **aren't good**, workers get **dissatisfied**.

2) **Motivating factors** are things like **interesting work**, personal **achievement**, **recognition** of achievement, and scope for more **responsibility** and personal **development**. These factors **do** positively motivate workers.

Motivating the Workforce

Financial Incentives are used to Reward and Motivate

Most people get paid a monthly **salary** or a weekly **wage**, but there are other kinds of financial motivation, too.

1) Workers who are paid a **weekly wage** get a set rate of so many **pounds per hour**. The more hours they work the more they get paid. There's a minimum wage — in 2007 it was £5.52 per hour for those aged 22 and over. Workers usually work a **fixed working week** of about 40 hours, and get paid more for any **overtime** they work.

2) Workers who get paid a monthly **salary** get a set amount per **year**, divided into 12 monthly payments. The salary isn't directly related to the number of hours worked — salaried employees work a minimum number of hours a week, and then as many hours as it takes to get the job done.

3) **Piecework** is where **production workers** are paid by **piece rate** — they get paid **per finished item** (or set quantity). The more the worker produces, the more they get paid.

4) Salespeople are usually paid **commission** — a **percentage** of the **sales** they achieve. Most sales staff get a low **basic salary** and earn commission on top of that, but some get commission only.

5) **Performance-related pay** gives more money to employees who meet their targets. Performance-related pay is linked to employee **appraisals** (interviews to find out how well an employee is doing). Some employees worry that they won't get a performance-related pay rise if they don't get on with the manager doing the appraisal interviews.

6) Employees may also get **fringe benefits**. These can include a **staff discount** for company products (common in retail, not so common in aircraft manufacturing...), employer contributions to employee **pensions**, private **medical insurance**, a company **car**, **profit-sharing** schemes or **shares** in the company.

7) Companies which have a **tall** structure are more likely to use **pay** to motivate people. **Communication** in tall structures can be **poor**, so it's **difficult** for them to use methods like **empowerment** and **consultation**.

Non-Financial Motivation — Jobs are Designed to be more Satisfying

Lots of businesses today design jobs to be motivating. A well-designed job has **varied job tasks** and gives employees some **control** over their work. It will also try to include as many of **Herzberg's motivating factors** as possible, e.g.:

1) **Job enlargement** gives the employee more work at the same level. It's also called **horizontal loading**.

2) **Job enrichment** gives workers more **challenging** work, and the **training** they need to do it. It gives employees more responsibility for organising their work and solving problems. It's also called **vertical loading**.

3) **Teamworking** puts workers into small teams and lets them organise their own work. In recent years, many firms have begun organising employees into teams, which is why organisational structures often include **team leaders**.

4) An organisation with a **flat** structure might **not** want to introduce **teamworking**, because having **team leaders** introduces an **extra** level of **hierarchy** and makes the structure taller.

5) **Empowerment** gives people more **control** over their work, and a greater role in **decision-making** — **quality circles** let groups of workers from various departments meet to suggest **improvements** to productivity and quality.

6) Organisations with a **flat** structure tend to be better at focusing on the **needs** of the **individual**, so they might motivate people through job **enlargement** or **enrichment**. **Communication** is **easier**, so staff are often involved in decision-making — **delegation** and **empowerment** are common.

Practice Questions

Q1 Give a brief description of Taylor's views on motivation.

Q2 Put the following needs in ascending order according to Maslow's hierarchy: friendship, job security, achievement.

Q3 Briefly explain the term "fringe benefits".

Q4 List and explain three non-financial motivators.

Exam Questions

Q1 A coffee-shop owner has a workforce made up of women with children, and part-time students. Explain how he could best increase motivation levels among his staff, giving reasons for your choices. (10 marks)

Q2 Colin is a checkout clerk in a supermarket, Jane is a travelling sales representative and Mike is a bricklayer. Say whether each person is likely to be paid by piece rate, hourly rate or commission, and explain why. (15 marks)

Sandwiches with Mayo increase productivity — no, really, they do...

It's the social factor, you see — people like eating them together. Right, back to the point... the theories of motivation. You won't be tested on who said what, but the ideas might well come in handy for giving examples of how managers today could increase the motivation of their workforce. Believe it or not, people aren't just in it for the money — no, really...

Capacity Utilisation

Changes in capacity utilisation affect a firm's ability to meet targets and impact on its break-even point and profit levels.

Capacity is Maximum Output with the Resources Currently Available

1) The **capacity** of an organisation is the **maximum** output that it can produce in a given period without buying any more fixed assets — machinery, factory space, etc.

2) Capacity depends on the **number of employees** and how skilled they are.

3) Capacity depends on the **technology** the business has — what **machinery** they have, what state it's in, what kind of computer system they have, etc.

4) Capacity depends on the kind of production **process** the business uses.

5) The amount of **investment** in the business is also a factor.

Check out the capacity on that...

Capacity Utilisation

Capacity utilisation is how much **capacity** a business is **using**. The following formula can be used to calculate it:

$$\text{Capacity Utilisation} = \frac{\text{Output}}{\text{Capacity}} \times 100\%$$

Example: a hotel with half its rooms booked out has a **capacity utilisation** of **50%**. A clothing factory with an output of 70 000 shirts per month and a maximum capacity of 100 000 shirts is running at **70%** capacity utilisation.

90% Capacity Utilisation is better than 100% Capacity Utilisation

High capacity utilisation is better than low capacity utilisation. However, 100% capacity utilisation has drawbacks.

1) Businesses have to consider all their **operational targets** when they plan their capacity usage. **Cost** isn't the only thing to think about — it might not be possible to operate at 100% capacity and keep **quality** levels high.

2) The business may have to turn away potential **customers**.

3) There's no **downtime** — machines are on **all the time**. If a machine has a problem, it'll cause delays as work piles up waiting for it to be fixed. There's no time for equipment maintenance, which can reduce the life of machinery.

4) There's no **margin of error**. Everything has to be perfect first time, which causes **stress** to managers. **Mistakes** are more likely when everyone's working flat out.

5) The business can't **temporarily increase output** for seasonal demand or one-off orders.

6) If output is greater than demand, there'll be **surplus stock** hanging about waiting to be sold. It's not good to have valuable **working capital** tied up in stock.

Businesses should plan production levels to achieve almost full capacity utilisation.

Firms can Increase their Capacity if they reach 100% capacity utilisation

Firms which are operating at full capacity don't just stop accepting new orders. They have ways of **increasing** their **capacity** so that they can **match** their **output** to **demand**. The best way to do this depends on whether the rise in demand is expected to be **temporary** or **long-term**.

1) Businesses can use **more capacity** by using their facilities for **more** of the **working week**. They can have staff working in two or three **shifts** in a day, and on weekends and bank holidays.

2) Businesses can buy **more machines**, if they can afford them (and the staff needed to operate them).

3) Businesses can **increase** their **staff levels** in the long run by recruiting new permanent staff. In the short run they can employ **temporary staff**, **part-time staff**, or get their staff to work **overtime**.

4) Businesses can also increase their capacity utilisation by increasing **productivity**. They can reorganise production by reallocating staff to the busiest areas, and they can increase employee **motivation**.

Firms can respond to unexpected Rises in Demand by Subcontracting work

1) **Subcontracting** is when a firm uses its **facilities** to do work on behalf of **another business**. E.g. a manufacturer of detergent might make detergent for a **supermarket** and package it with the supermarket's own label.

2) Companies can **subcontract** work to other businesses in **busy periods**. This means they can meet **unexpected increases in demand** without increasing their own capacity and having the costs of extra staff and facilities all year round.

Capacity Utilisation

Under-utilisation is Inefficient and increases Unit Costs

Low capacity utilisation is called **under-utilisation**. It's **inefficient** because it means a business is **not** getting **use** out of **machines** and **facilities** that have been paid for.

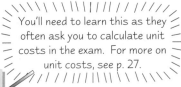

You'll need to learn this as they often ask you to calculate unit costs in the exam. For more on unit costs, see p. 27.

1) Under-utilisation increases costs because it causes fixed costs to be spread over less output, so unit costs increase.

2) Higher capacity utilisation creates **economies of scale**, which means a **decrease** in **variable costs**.

$$\text{Unit cost} = \frac{\text{Total Costs}}{\text{Output}}$$

> **Example:** A chocolate factory's total costs are £7200 a month. In November, the factory output 18 000 chocolate bars, giving a unit cost of £0.40. In December, absenteeism caused output to fall to 16 000 bars, meaning that the unit cost rose to £0.45.

Firms with Low Demand should try to Reduce Capacity

Sometimes firms have **too much capacity** and **not enough demand** for their product, which leads to **under-utilisation**. When this happens, they'll **first** try to **increase demand**, but if that doesn't work, they need to **reduce capacity**.

1) Businesses stimulate demand by changing the **marketing mix**. They can change the **promotion** of a product, or change its **price** or its **distribution** (see p.59-71 for more on the marketing mix).

2) Businesses can also fill spare capacity by **subcontracting** work for other firms (see p.46). It's better to make goods for a **competitor** and make a bit of money than it is to leave **machinery** sitting around doing **nothing**.

3) If a business can't increase demand for their product, they need to **reduce their capacity** by closing part of their production facilities. This is called **rationalisation** (or **downsizing**). It's become popular with large firms who want to stay competitive by cutting their production costs.

4) Businesses can reduce capacity in the **short term** by stopping **overtime** or reducing the length of the working week, allocating staff to **other work** in the business, and by not renewing **temporary contracts**.

5) Businesses can reduce capacity in the **long term** by not **replacing** staff as they retire (natural wastage), making staff **redundant**, and by **selling off** factories or equipment.

Firms have to consider how their Capacity Needs will Change over Time

1) Demand **changes** over time, so firms must think about demand in the **future** as well as the current demand.

2) The key to **long-term** success is planning **capacity** changes to match long-term changes in demand, but this can be tricky. You can use market research to help predict future demand, but it's not 100% certain. There's always an element of risk.

3) **Short-term** changes in **capacity utilisation** provide **flexibility**. Firms should be flexible and **temporarily** increase existing capacity utilisation if an increase in demand isn't expected to continue **long-term** — e.g with seasonal goods like Christmas crackers, goods heading towards decline in their life cycle, and one-off special orders.

4) **Long-term** solutions end up giving **lower unit costs** — as long as **predictions** of demand turn out to be **true**.

Practice Questions

Q1 Calculate capacity utilisation for a restaurant that has 65 seats but only 42 people dining each night.

Q2 Give three ways in which a firm can increase its output to meet an increase in orders. Answers on p. 78.

Q3 Calculate how much it costs to produce one shirt, if a factory is making 450 a month and has total monthly costs of £1600.

Q4 Explain what is meant by "rationalisation".

Exam Questions

Q1 Discuss why 95% capacity utilisation is considered better for a firm than 100%. (4 marks)

Q2 Analyse how a manufacturer of fashion clothing should expand their business if recent growth has led to capacity utilisation reaching 100%. (10 marks)

She cannae take any more, Jim...

Capacity utilisation crops up elsewhere. Under-utilisation is a consequence of low demand. When a business launches a product, capacity utilisation starts out low and then builds up as demand for the new product increases. It really is very much worth your while to know how businesses take action to get their capacity utilisation to around the 90% mark.

Quality

Increased competition means that firms now compete through quality as well as price.
High quality increases revenues and reduces costs.

Good Quality products and services Meet Customer Needs

1) Products have to be **fit** for the **purpose** they're made for. For example, the quality of a tin-opener is judged by how well it opens tins.

2) The **customer's opinion** of quality is the most important one. Businesses should use **market research** to check customers are satisfied with product quality.

High Quality Increases Profits

1) In the **dark old days**, managers thought quality improvements **increased costs**, so they only went for **slight** quality improvements which wouldn't cost very much.

2) Enlightened managers think of the **opportunity cost** of **not** having a great quality product. They go for high quality as a way of actually **reducing costs** and increasing revenue.

Quality improvements reduce costs:

1) Less **raw materials** and less **worker** and **machinery** time get used up by **mistakes**.
2) You don't need as much **advertising** and **promotional** gubbins to persuade **shops** to stock high quality goods.
3) You don't need to spend as much on **marketing** to attract **new customers**.
4) You need fewer **customer care staff** because there aren't as many **complaints** to deal with.
5) There are fewer **refunds** and fewer claims on **warranties**.

Quality improvements increase revenue:

1) You don't need to **discount** prices to sell **damaged stock** when there isn't any damaged or "seconds" quality stock.
2) You have greater price flexibility — high quality products allow for **premium pricing**.
3) Quality is a way of differentiating your product from the competition — it can function as a **unique selling point (USP)**.
4) High quality products improve the **image** and **reputation** of the business.
5) Quality goods and services make it easy to keep **existing customers**.
6) A good reputation for quality brings in **new customers**.

Self-checking can be more Motivating than Inspection

1) The traditional **quality control** approach assumes that errors are **unavoidable**. It says that the best you can do is to **detect errors** and **put them right** before customers buy the products.

2) Traditionally, **quality control inspectors** checked other people's work. This has drawbacks — inspectors are additional staff and need to be paid, and employees feel distrusted and demotivated.

3) **Quality assurance** is a more modern approach to quality control. With quality assurance, workers check their own work. This is called **self-checking**. **Empowering** employees to check the quality of their own work can be highly **motivating**.

4) Under a self-checking system, it's **everyone's responsibility** to produce good work. Everyone should try to get it **right first time**. Workers can **reject** components or work in progress if they're not up to standard. They don't pass the poor quality off as **someone else's problem**. Workers are responsible for passing on good quality work in progress to the next stage of the production process.

5) **Training** is really important for quality assurance. Workers have to be trained to produce good quality products and services. New recruits get this as part of their **induction**. Experienced workers might need **retraining** from time to time.

6) Workers must be **motivated** and **committed** to quality for quality assurance schemes to work.

7) The ultimate aim of quality assurance is to create a culture of **zero defects**.

Quality

Total Quality Management is the Ultimate version of Quality Assurance

1) **Total Quality Management** (TQM) means the **whole workforce** has to be committed to quality improvements. The idea is to **build quality** into every department and not let quality get squeezed out.

2) With TQM, every employee has to try to **satisfy customers** — and everybody that they work for must be thought of as a customer, even fellow employees. So both **external** customers that the business sells things to, and **internal** customers within the business, must receive a quality service.

3) It takes **time** to introduce TQM — workers need **training** so that they see quality as their responsibility. This can be **expensive** and **disrupt production** in the short-term. It can also seem like a lot of extra work, which can be **demotivating** for employees. Some companies that use TQM motivate their staff by **rewarding** quality.

Quality Awards are Evidence of High Standards

1) **BS 5750** is an award given out by the **British Standards Institution** to firms with good quality assurance systems which meet the industry standard. **ISO 9000** is the **European** quality award. It's equivalent to BS 5750.

2) To get the award, a business must set **quality targets**, make sure their production process **achieves** these targets, and continually **monitor** production quality. This process can **cost money**.

3) The British Standards Institute **don't care** too much what the business' quality targets actually are, only that they meet the **industry standard** and have systems in place to meet their own targets.

4) BS 5750 and ISO 9000 can be used in **marketing** to win the trust of customers.

They couldn't understand what had happened to their quality award.

Practice Questions

Q1 Give two reasons why high quality reduces costs.

Q2 What's the difference between quality control and quality assurance?

Q3 What must a business do in order to get a BS 5750 award?

Exam Questions

Q1 Examine the potential costs and benefits of obtaining ISO 9000 certification. (8 marks)

Q2 The Managing Director of Ropey Textiles decides to introduce Total Quality Management to the business. Explain why employees may be resistant to TQM, and suggest how it might be successfully introduced. (10 marks)

AS Examiners — the ultimate quality control inspectors...

It's pretty obvious that good quality is important in business. People don't like paying for things that aren't any good. There are different ways to go about making sure that products and services are of good quality — one important difference is between quality control inspections of finished products and quality assurance systems for the whole production process.

Customer Service

Providing good customer service is one thing that makes businesses competitive in the long term. If a business is committed to providing good service, it needs to spend a lot of money and time developing a quality culture.

Customers **Expect** good service from a **Company**

Basically, customer service means providing a service or product in the way that has been promised.

1) **Customer service** is the **actions** that a business takes to **keep** its **customers happy**. Customer service can be part of the sales process **before**, **during**, or **after** the sale itself.

2) Having a customer service **philosophy** means admitting to mistakes and dealing with complaints — customers like companies to admit when they're wrong, explain the problem and make amends. An important part of the process is making **customer service** part of the organisation's **culture**, and ensuring that all **employees** work hard to provide **excellent** levels of **customer service**.

3) Knowing the customer is **vital** to good customer service. A company has to know what its customers **want** and **expect** in order to be able to provide it — that's why **market research** (p.12) and **feedback** are so important. Companies can get feedback through guestbooks, questionnaires, **secret shoppers** (customers who are paid to use a service to provide feedback on it) and emails.

4) The way companies deliver customer service is **changing**. Email and chat systems make it easy for customers to speak to experts at **any time**, and call centres can handle **hundreds** of customers per hour. These developments have also made senior management more **directly involved** in customer services — in some cases (e.g. service stations) you can directly telephone the **manager** to complain.

Good Customer Service gives companies a **Competitive Advantage**

Providing good customer service uses up **time** and **money**. There are plenty of reasons why many companies think it's still **worth** making the **effort**, though...

1) Good customer service can provide a **USP** (Unique Selling Point, see p.60).

2) Customers can now shop 24 hours a day, online or by phone, and expect to be able to buy products **quickly** and **easily**. Since many companies provide identical products at similar prices, most customers will go to one that offers high levels of **service** that are **consistently delivered**.

3) New products, services and technological improvements can be copied by the competition, but a good **service reputation** is **hard** to **duplicate**.

4) Companies that provide added value and superior customer service can **charge more** than their competitors.

5) **Long-term customers** buy more, take less company time, bring in new customers and are less price sensitive (put off by price rises). Companies now look at customers in terms of their **LTV** (Lifetime Value) to the company.

6) **Satisfied customers** are the best **advert** for the company as they spread its reputation by **word of mouth**.

In a world dominated by Chip and Pin technology, giving customers the chance to sign for goods was a unique customer service.

Good customer service → Happy customer → Repeat purchase → Better profits → Company competes more effectively

Customer Service

Different Types of Business offer Different Types of Customer Service

The way in which a business provides service depends on what type of business it is.
However, most businesses offer some form of these three basic aspects of customer service:

1) Products and services need to be **customer-focused** and provide **value** for money.

2) Businesses have to treat customers as individuals with **different needs**.

3) **After-sales service** — following up with after-sales support such as maintenance.

Companies who want to get a **competitive advantage** from customer service often try to **go beyond** the types of service listed above. **How** they go about this depends on what type of business they are:

1) Businesses such as shops, where the customer comes **face to face** with staff, are likely to invest in **staff training**. **Extended opening hours** and **home delivery** might also improve customer satisfaction.

2) **Online** and **telephone retailers** don't deal with the customer face to face, so they have to find other ways of giving good customer service. Some have customer service **call centres** that are open **long hours**. Others offer **next-day** or **free delivery** or are more **flexible** about **returning** goods.

3) **Business to Business (B2B)** companies (see p.57) focus their customer service efforts on building **long-term relationships** with their **clients**, often by providing spare parts or maintenance. This is because businesses that sell to businesses usually have a **few clients** who each spend **lots** of **money**, whereas firms that sell to private customers have a lot of customers each spending relatively small amounts of money.

Research, Training and Quality Management all Improve Customer Service

Companies are always trying to monitor and improve the level of customer service that they offer.
They do this by investing in market research and training and by introducing quality management systems.

1) **Market research** involves gathering and analysing information about customers through **customer surveys** and **questionnaires**. Managers can use this information to help them **understand** the **market** and make sure products and services meet the **customer's needs**. Look back at page 12 for more on market research.

2) Staff should be **knowledgeable** about the product or service they are selling. Companies use **training** to make sure employees have this knowledge. Training can also be used to ensure that staff have a **positive attitude** towards the customer.

3) **Quality systems** ensure that products and services are **produced** and **sold** at an acceptable **standard** and **quality**. Firms can use methods of **quality assurance** such as **Total Quality Management** (TQM, see p.49) to create a quality culture and make sure all employees are contributing in some way to customer service targets. Alternatively, they might introduce **quality standards** such as ISO 9000 (see page 49).

Quality culture.

Practice Questions

Q1 How would you define customer service?

Q2 Why is it beneficial for a company to have long-term customers?

Q3 What factors contribute to high levels of customer satisfaction?

Q4 How can a company benefit from satisfying customer needs?

Exam Question

Q1 a) Discuss the alternatives a company has for developing its customer service. (10 marks)

b) Analyse the benefits it might gain as a result of improving its customer service. (6 marks)

All our writers are currently busy — please continue to hold...

When you've been waiting for someone to answer your call for an hour, it's easy to feel like companies don't care about customer service at all. But it costs them as much to win one new customer as it does to keep five existing ones. So, believe it or not, they're usually doing everything in their power to keep you sweet. Make sure you learn how they do it.

Suppliers

It's not called a supply chain for nothin' — every business in the chain needs to pull their weight, or production just doesn't happen...

Producing **High Quality** products **Depends** on **Good Suppliers**

A company's **performance** is often **linked** to the activities and performance of its **suppliers**.

1) A **supply chain** consists of the group of **firms** that are involved in **all** the various **processes** required to make a **finished product / service** available to the customer.

2) The chain **begins** with the provider of **raw materials** and **ends** with the firm that sells the **finished product**.

3) The members of a supply chain will **vary** depending on the type of product/service, but will typically include **suppliers**, **manufacturers**, **distributors** and **retailers**.

4) **All** the **members** of the supply chain need to **function efficiently**. If any of them are unreliable, the product won't be on the shelves when it needs to be, or the quality will be poor, which reflects badly on the company producing it.

"We should be able to get those components to you by 1952."

Companies need to consider **Price** and **Reliability** when **Choosing a Supplier**

The most **effective suppliers** are those who offer products or services that **match** (or **exceed**) the **needs** of your business. So when you are looking for **suppliers**, it's best to be **sure** of your **business needs** and what you want to achieve. The most important factors to consider are:

Price	The **total cost** of acquiring the product. Firms have to decide **how much** they are willing to pay and whether **cost** is their **first priority**. If they want to cut down the time it takes to serve customers, suppliers that offer faster delivery will rate higher than those that compete on price alone.
Payment Terms	Companies need to know **how much** they need to pay, **how** it has to be paid and **when** it should be paid by. **Small suppliers** may only be able to offer **30 days' credit**, as they often have poor cash flow. Some **larger firms** may be able to offer as much as **120 days'** credit.
Quality	The **quality** of supplies needs to be **consistent** — customers associate **poor quality** with the business they buy from, not their suppliers.
Capacity	Businesses need to select **suppliers** who are able to **meet** any **peaks** in **demand** for particular products / services.
Reliability	If **a supplier** lets a **firm** down, that firm may not be able to supply its **own** customers. Suppliers need to **deliver on time**, or give plenty of **warning** if they can't.
Flexibility	**Suppliers** need to be able to **respond easily** to **changes** in a company's **requirements**. Efficient production relies on suppliers who can provide extra (or fewer) supplies at **short notice**.

Companies build **Relationships** with their **Suppliers**

A **strategic working relationship** is one where both companies in the relationship can get **long-term benefits** from **working together**. There are several ways for companies to build strategic working relationships with their suppliers:

1) **Linked Networks** — **shared IT systems** such as inventory (stock) control management allow both the company and its supplier to view stock levels, so they both know in plenty of time when more supplies will be needed. This can improve **efficiency**, cut **costs**, and improve **customer value**.

2) **JIT (Just-in-Time) Systems** — these are becoming a popular way of managing operations. The goal of JIT systems is to have only the **right amounts** of **materials** arrive at precisely the **times** they are **needed**. Because supplies arrive just as they are needed you don't need a big warehouse, and there's **less waste**.

3) **Shared Costs** — if a business and its supplier are producing similar goods, there's a good chance they'll be able to save money by sharing **specialist equipment** and storing their goods in the same **warehouse**.

Suppliers

A *Well-managed Supply Chain* can *Improve Operational Performance*

1) If a business **works** closely with the **right suppliers**, there's a good chance that **operational performance** will **improve**.

2) **Productivity** will **increase**, which causes **costs** to **fall** (for more on the link between these two, see p.40).

3) Also, a business with an **efficient supply chain** is in a much better position to meet its customers' expectations.

Mr MacDonald and Mr Paulin had spent three days choosing a supplier for a new stapler.

> 1) A company's buyers need to make sure that they **only buy** the **supplies** that the **company** really **needs** — they mustn't be wowed by slick sales pitches.

> 2) They also need to understand the difference between a **strategic supplier**, who provides goods or services that are essential to the business — such as high-value raw materials, and a **non-strategic supplier** who provides low-value supplies such as office stationery. It's important to spend **more time** selecting and managing **strategic suppliers** than non-strategic suppliers.

> 3) It's often easier, and generally more **cost-effective**, for businesses to **limit** the number of **sources** they buy from. However, it's **dangerous** to have just **one supplier** because if there are ever problems with that supplier, the business has nowhere to turn.

> 4) It's always worth having an **alternative supply source** ready to help in difficult times. This is really important for suppliers who are essential to the success of the business.

Practice Questions

Q1 Give three types of company that you would expect to find as part of a supply chain.
Q2 Why would a business choose a JIT method of production?
Q3 What is the difference between a strategic supplier and a non-strategic supplier?
Q4 Why is it risky for a business to rely on a single supplier?

Exam Questions

Q1 Alpha Ironmonger Ltd is looking for a supplier of beef to use in its new range of beef pies. Discuss the factors it should consider before deciding which one to choose. (8 marks)

Q2 Mr Brown, director of Browns Brushes Ltd, wants to improve his relationship with his suppliers. Discuss the ways in which he could achieve this. (8 marks)

Supply me to the moon, let me sing among the stock...

If you're a business, the relationship with your supplier might be the best one you'll ever have. Or the worst. If your suppliers do what they're supposed to when they're supposed to, there's a good chance that the production process will all run to plan. If they're late, or just don't deliver, production stops, staff have absolutely nowt to do — it's a disaster, basically...

Technology in Operations

Most modern businesses rely heavily on technology, from automated production lines to computer systems. Technology can make a firm more cost-effective and efficient, but it needs constant updating and maintenance.

Businesses use *Two* main types of *Technology*

The main technologies that companies use in day-to-day operations are:

1) **Robotic Engineering** — using robots as part of the manufacturing process.

2) **Computer Technology** — computers are used by businesses in lots of different ways. Product development, business communications and finance departments all depend heavily on IT systems.

Using *Robots* can *Reduce Staffing Costs*

1) **Robots** are mostly used to replace human staff for **tasks** which are **dangerous**, **repetitive** or **boring**.

2) **Factories** and **production plants** often use **automated pickers** to take goods from the production line and pack them into boxes. It's usually **cheaper** and **faster** for robots to do this job instead of humans.

3) Companies that are planning to replace human workers with robots need to weigh up the **advantages** of using robots against the **demotivating effect** that it is likely to have on staff.

Advantages of using Robots	1) Company needs **fewer employees**, so staff **costs fall**. 2) Robots are generally more **accurate** — human error is eliminated. 3) Robots are more **reliable** than human workers. 4) Robots can be used for **tasks** that could be **unsafe** for **humans**, e.g. bomb detection.
Disadvantages of using Robots	1) Some **staff** may **lose** their **jobs**, which can be **demotivating** for colleagues. 2) **Incorrect programming** can lead to **errors** being made. 3) **High initial cost** involved in **purchasing** robot. 4) **Maintenance** costs can be **expensive**.

Luke claimed to be developing a new robot. His colleagues thought he was just playing chess.

IT helps make *Companies* more *Efficient*

1) **Computer-aided design** (CAD) uses computers to design new products, or make alterations to existing products. CAD produces 3D mock-ups on screen — managers don't have to wait for a **prototype** (model) to be built before they know what the product will look like. This can also be useful for marketing things like new kitchens.

2) **Computer-aided manufacture** (CAM) uses computers to produce a product, usually involving **robots** or 'computer-numerically controlled' (CNC) machines — automatic lathes which form a material into a finished product from a computer design. CAM is often combined with the CAD process — products are designed on computer, and the design data fed straight into the production machine. This is called **CAD/CAM**.

3) Computers make **stock control** easier. Holding stock information in a database makes it much easier to monitor when you need to order new stock. In retailing this is often combined with **Electronic Point of Sale (EPOS)** systems that rely on barcodes to record which products are being purchased by customers. This means stocks can be re-ordered automatically. Having a good stock control system makes it easier for companies such as supermarkets and big retailers to move to a **just-in-time** supply system (see p.52).

4) **IT** helps with **budgetary control**. The finance department can easily compare current expenditure levels with original budgets using **spreadsheets**.

5) Spreadsheets allow managers to investigate "what if?" scenarios. They can calculate the impact of **potential changes** in expenditure or sales, which makes **decision-making** easier.

IT helps make *Communication Faster* and more *Effective*

Information can be shared **within** the **company** using an **intranet**. Businesses communicate with other **businesses** and with **customers** by **fax**, **email** and the **internet**.

1) Email is a fast and efficient method of communicating, both internally and externally.

2) The **internet** allows businesses to reach a **larger customer base**, and do business **24 hours a day**. Customers can check a business' **website** for information rather than phoning a helpline or sending a letter in the post.

Technology in Operations

Marketing departments use Technology to gather Information about Customers

Many companies now use **technology** to gather **information** about the **lifestyles** of their **customers** and the **products** that they **buy** or are likely to buy. This helps them to make sure that **promotions** are **targeting** the right people and will actually cause **sales** to **increase**.

1) Lots of supermarkets offer **loyalty cards** which give customers money back according to how much they spend. One **benefit** for the supermarket is that it allows them to form a **database** of customer names and addresses which they can then use to create **mailing lists** for **direct marketing** campaigns.

2) **Loyalty cards** also tell the supermarkets what **products** a particular customer is **buying**. This means they can send out **offers** which **relate** to the kind of products that the person buys **most often**.

3) **Social networking websites** are another way that businesses can use technology to find out more about customer likes and dislikes. People who use these sites often list information about themselves, including the type of **music** they like, where they go on **holiday**, what **car** they drive etc. Companies who advertise on these sites can make their adverts visible only to the people who are **likely** to **buy** their product — this is **cheaper** and more **effective** than targeting everyone who uses the website. **Search engines** like Google™ often use targeted advertising — they show adverts that are **relevant** to the topic the user searched for.

Firms need to consider the Advantages and Disadvantages of Technology

Most companies invest a lot of money in technology. Technology is beneficial if it leads to:

1) **Increased productivity** — machines can often do tasks quicker than humans can.
2) Improved **quality**.
3) **Reduced waste** through more effective production methods.
4) More **effective** and **efficient delivery** of goods and services to the customer.
5) More **effective marketing** campaigns that target the right customers.
6) More productive **staff utilisation** — staff can be transferred to more urgent or complicated tasks.
7) **Reduced** administrative and financial **costs**.
8) **Better communications** both internally and externally.

However, introducing new technology or updating older systems can create problems:

1) **Initial costs** of technology may be **high**.
2) Technology requires **constant updating** in order to stay current, which can also be **expensive**.
3) New IT systems may create an **increased** need for **staff training**.

Practice Questions

Q1 What is meant by CAD? How can a business use it?
Q2 Give two advantages and two disadvantages of using robots.
Q3 How can social networking websites be beneficial to marketing departments?
Q4 Give two advantages and two disadvantages of using technology in business.

Exam Question

Q1 (a) Identify three areas where technology may be utilised in a company. (3 marks)

(b) Discuss how technology can be used in each of these areas to benefit the company. (12 marks)

If these pages are repetitive and boring — they're the work of a robot...

Reading through this lot is enough to make you wonder how businesses ever coped before technology came along. You need to know the two main types of technology that businesses use today, as well as the benefits and pitfalls of using technology. Robots might be cheaper than humans, but they tell lousy jokes, don't flirt, and are no good at making tea...

Effective Marketing

Marketing is "the management process responsible for identifying, anticipating and satisfying consumer requirements profitably." Well, that's what the Chartered Institute of Marketing says — I suppose they'd know.

Marketing identifies customer Needs and Wants

1) Marketing finds out what customers **need and want**. Marketing also tries to **anticipate** what they'll want in the future so that the business can get **one step ahead** of the market.

2) Marketing tries to ensure that the business supplies **goods and services** that customers **want** in order to **make a profit**. It's mutually beneficial — the customer gets something they want, the business makes a profit.

3) Marketing covers **research**, **analysis**, **planning** and the **"marketing mix"**. The "marketing mix" is all the decisions a business makes about promoting and selling a product.

4) Most larger businesses have a specialised **marketing department** — but marketing affects all departments.

Marketing is important in a Competitive Environment

1) Companies selling goods in a competitive environment rely on **marketing** to help them **obtain** a **share** of the **market**.

2) Once they have a customer base, marketing (especially **market research**) helps them come up with **new products** and make sure that their **customers** don't **shop elsewhere**.

3) Companies invent **unique selling points** (USPs) for their products to persuade customers to buy their products rather than products from a competitor (there's more on USPs on p.60).

4) **Marketing** helps make sure that **customers** stay **loyal** to a particular **brand** (see p.64 for more on branding).

High Disposable Income increases the Need for Marketing

1) **Disposable income** is the amount of money that consumers have left to spend **after** they have paid **taxes** and **pension** contributions. It tends to go up and down depending on whether the economy is strong or weak.

2) When consumers have **lots** of disposable income, they start to **buy things** they **wouldn't usually** buy — such as luxury and designer goods.

3) Manufacturers of these types of product all want to attract a **share** of this new group of customers, so they **increase** the amount that they spend on **marketing**.

4) This extra spending on marketing causes sales to rise, which leads to an **increase** in **revenue**.

5) The combination of increased revenue and a wider market means companies might consider **new forms** of **advertising** which target a bigger group of people — e.g. a national women's magazine, or billboards.

6) However, an increase in disposable income can also lead to a **decrease** in demand for **cheaper**, lower quality **products**. Manufacturers of these products might spend **more** on **marketing** to win back market share.

Globalisation and Brand Awareness can affect Marketing Strategy

1) In general, **globalisation** is **good** for **large companies**, because it allows them to sell their product all over the world. **Coca-Cola®** and **McDonald's** are examples of very successful **global brands**.

2) The global market has led to **customers** being very **brand aware**. Companies often **market** major brands **differently** from the way that they market lesser-known products.

3) Successful brands, such as Cadbury, often choose to **advertise** the **brand name**, rather than a specific product. The advantage of this is that it **increases** the sales of **all** their products, not just one in particular.

4) The producers of **successful** brands tend to have a lot of **influence**. This makes it easier for them to persuade **retailers** to install special point of sale displays (for more on point of sale, see p.65) and gives them access to extremely high profile forms of advertising, such as **product placement** in films.

5) Some consumers **dislike** buying from large, **global companies**, because they feel that they are impersonal or too powerful. This has led some companies, such as HSBC, to adopt **marketing** campaigns which **emphasise** their ability to adapt to the **local** environment.

Effective Marketing

Marketing can be aimed at Large or Small Groups of Consumers

Mass marketing is a way of trying to make sure that **as many** customers **as possible** see a particular product. **Niche marketing** tries to sell to a **smaller**, more **specific** group of people. More on niche and mass markets on p.8 and p.10.

Advantages of Niche Marketing

+   Niche marketing **only** targets people who are likely to be **interested** in the product in question. So although it only reaches a small group of consumers, there is a good chance they will want to buy the product.

+   Because it only targets a very limited group of customers, niche marketing is **cheaper** than mass marketing.

Disadvantages of Niche Marketing

–   Some companies selling to a niche market are forced to set a **high price** for their product. This is because their low levels of production prevent them benefiting from **economies of scale**.

–   Another disadvantage of niche marketing is that identifying a niche can be **expensive**, as well as **time-consuming**.

Advantages of Mass Marketing

+   The most obvious advantage of mass marketing is that it allows companies to reach a **huge audience**.

+   Producers of mass market products save money because of **economies of scale**. These savings can be passed on to consumers, allowing firms to **compete** on **price**.

Disadvantages of Mass Marketing

–   A mass marketing strategy is unlikely to make customers feel that a product meets their **exact needs**. **Market share** can **decrease** as niche products break the market into smaller segments.

–   Mass marketing is **expensive**, as it relies on **widespread forms** of promotion, such as TV advertising.

Companies can use Marketing to target Customers or Other Businesses

The growth of the internet has created many new types of business. Two of the most important of these are **business-to-business** (B2B) companies, and **business-to-consumer** (B2C) companies.

With a name like B2C they would never have reached the top 40, even without the pink trumpet.

1)   B2B companies sell to other **businesses**. They usually sell **services**, such as help with recruitment, or **telecommunications** and **computer products**.

2)   B2C businesses, such as Amazon.com®, sell goods **directly** to the **public** via the internet.

3)   B2B marketing tries to **build** a **long-term relationship** with the consumer. It emphasises **after-sales service**.

4)   B2C companies use **discounts**, **advertising** and other **promotions** to persuade people to **spend money**.

Practice Questions

Q1   What is meant by "disposable income"?

Q2   Give three ways in which increased brand awareness has changed the way that businesses market goods.

Q3   What kind of services and products do B2B businesses usually sell?

Exam Questions

Q1   Explain how changes in disposable income can increase the need for marketing.   (5 marks)

Q2   Justify why a business selling tie-dye T-shirts should consider a niche marketing strategy.   (4 marks)

Maybe I'll find a niche, crawl into it, and stay there forever...

You might feel like you can't get away from all this marketing stuff — companies probably feel that way too. When customers are spending more money, companies need marketing to persuade them to spend it on their products. When they spend less, marketing tries to tempt them to keep buying. If only consumers weren't such a fickle bunch...

Managing a Range of Products

There's a lot to think about before bringing a new product onto the market. Businesses need the right mix of new, growing and mature products to survive in the long-term. And the wrong product can be a pricey mistake.

Businesses need a *Variety* of *Products* — a *Mixed Product Portfolio*

1) A **product line** consists of related products with similar characteristics, uses or target customers.

2) The **product mix** is the **combination** of all the **product lines** that a business produces.

The product mix is also called the product portfolio.

3) Businesses aim to have a **product mix** that contains a variety of different products, all at different stages of the product life cycle (see p.62). That way if one product fails, the business should still be able to depend on the others.

The *Boston Matrix* is a model of *Portfolio Analysis*

The Boston Matrix compares **market growth** with **market share**. Each **circle** in the matrix represents **one product**. The **size** of each circle represents the **sales revenue** of the product.

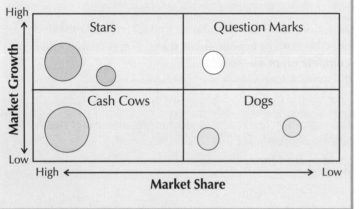

1) All **new products** are **question marks** (sometimes called **problem children** or **wildcats**) and they have small market share and high market growth. These aren't profitable yet and could succeed or fail. They need **heavy marketing** to give them a chance. A business can do various things with question marks — **brand building**, **harvesting** (maximising sales or profit in the short term) or **divestment** (selling off the product).

2) **Stars** have high market growth and high market share. They're in their profitable **growth** phase and have the most potential. They're future cash cows.

3) **Cash cows** have high market share but low market growth. They're in their **maturity** phase. They've already been promoted and they're produced in high volumes, so costs are low. Cash cows bring in plenty of **money**.

Jack had low growth — so he tried standing on two legs to make himself look taller.

4) **Dogs** have low market share and low market growth. They're usually pretty much a lost cause. If they're still profitable, e.g. a chocolate bar that is still popular, but no longer growing, the business will **harvest profit** in the **short term**. If the product is no longer making a profit it can be **sold off**.

The *Boston Matrix* is a useful tool

1) The Boston Matrix lets a business see if it has a good balanced **product portfolio**. A balanced product portfolio means that a business can use money from its **cash cows** to **invest** in its **question marks** so they can become **stars**. Because the products are all related in this way, it's important to take them all into account when making decisions.

2) The Boston Matrix **can't** always **predict exactly** what will happen to a product. A product's **cash flow** and **profit** may be **different** from what the matrix suggests (e.g. a dog may have strong cash flow and be profitable despite falling sales).

Managing a Range of Products

The *Marketing Mix* — *Product*, *Price*, *Place*, *Promotion*

The marketing mix describes the **factors** that firms consider when **marketing** a product. It's often known as **the 4 Ps**.

1) The marketing mix is the combination of factors that **affect a customer's decision** to buy. The **price** has to be right, the **product** has to be right, the product must be distributed to the right **places**, and it has to be **promoted** in the right way. **Market research** helps companies put together a marketing mix that works.

> A marketing mix with factors which work well together is called an integrated marketing mix.

2) The factors in the marketing mix have to **work together**. E.g. if a company develops a very exclusive product, which it then distributes to shops all over the country, then the easy availability of the product could cause it to lose its exclusivity, which might discourage people from buying it. But businesses also have to **compromise** — it would be unusual for a **niche product** produced by a small firm to have a high enough marketing budget to allow for TV adverts, promotional pricing and point-of-sale displays, so the **marketing department** has to **decide** which of these they think will be **most effective**.

3) A business has to be **realistic** when it's putting together its marketing mix. E.g. a business that's based in Alaska might not be able to include next-day delivery to the rest of the world in its mix.

The Marketing Mix is influenced by the *Marketing Environment*

The marketing mix needs to be **constantly reviewed** if a product is going to be successful in the long term, because the environment that surrounds the marketing mix changes all the time.

1) The **marketing environment** is made up of many **different forces** which influence the marketing mix. These forces might be **legal**, **financial**, **technological** or **political**.

2) It can be hard for companies to **predict** changes in the marketing environment. Most companies **react** to changes by **adapting** their marketing mix.

3) Companies might change their marketing mix as a result of new **market research**.

4) **Political** forces include **government taxes** — the government can raise or lower tax on things like cigarettes and alcohol in its annual **budget**.

5) **Legal** forces are designed to prevent **monopolies** (see p.72) and to **protect** the consumer. They stop companies from charging excessive prices or manufacturing **products** that could be dangerous, e.g. clothing made of flammable fabric.

Cindy thought the 4 Ps were Party, Party, Party, Party.

6) Advances in **technology** have two main effects. They influence the **type of products** that a company can offer and also cause **customers' aspirations** to change.

7) **Financial** or economic forces affect both **consumer** and **company** spending. In times of prosperity, both consumers and businesses spend more, whereas a **weak economy** (high interest rates, high unemployment etc.) causes consumers to cut back and forces businesses to cut costs, too.

8) **Social** factors, like an increasing number of pensioners, or more workers from Eastern Europe affect **demand** and **consumer spending** patterns.

9) Some changes in the marketing environment are **harmful** to certain companies, but **beneficial** to others. In the 1990s, when sales of beef were affected by BSE, sales of other meats rose as people changed their **buying habits**.

Practice Questions

Q1 What can a business do to its question marks to turn them into stars?
Q2 What is meant by "marketing mix"?
Q3 Give examples of ways in which changes in technology might influence the marketing mix.

Exam Questions

Q1 Discuss the usefulness of the Boston Matrix to a biscuit manufacturer. (10 marks)

Q2 A crisp manufacturer has just carried out market research which shows that consumers now want luxury crisps for dinner parties. Suggest how the firm might change its marketing mix in reaction to this. (8 marks)

Cash cows bring in plenty of money — but piggy banks do that too...

There's a lot for businesses to plan before they launch a new product — they have to be as sure as they can be that the product they've spent time and money on won't be a flop. Once it's gone from 'question mark' to 'cash cow,' they need to keep an eye on the marketing environment, and adjust the marketing mix to make sure the product stays profitable.

Marketing Mix: Product

Many marketing experts think that the product is the most important element of the marketing mix. Not everyone agrees, but companies do need to develop new goods and services in order to keep on being successful.

New Products can be great for a business

There are three main reasons why it is worthwhile for companies to develop new products:

1) New products can bring in **new customers**.
2) They give a **competitive** advantage.
3) They allow companies to maintain a **balanced product portfolio**.

Competition and Technology can inspire New Products

Most new products come about for one of three reasons:

1) **Technological developments** mean that a company can now offer the customer something that it couldn't offer before, e.g. a DVD player instead of a video player.

2) A company might develop a new product in response to one which has been launched by a **competitor**, e.g. lots of companies developed bagless vacuum cleaners after the launch of the Dyson™.

3) Somebody within the company (usually the owner or a manager) identifies a **gap in the market**. See page 12 for more on identifying gaps in the market.

There are Three Types of New Product

A product is considered to be 'new,' if it fits into one of the following categories:

1) **Innovative** — innovative products are completely original. Products such as Sony's Walkman® or 3M's Post-it® notes originally fitted into this category.

2) **Imitative** — these are products which copy innovative products once they have become successful. For example, there are now loads of different makes of portable CD player or sticky notes.

3) **Replacement** — a new model of an existing product is developed and the old one is phased out.

1) In order to create **innovative products**, companies have to spend lots of money on **research and development (R&D)**.

2) They also need a **proactive** approach to product development. This happens when a firm is attempting to be a **leader** and **create the market**. This strategy is **high risk**, but also carries the **highest potential rewards**.

Companies with innovative products often protect their ideas using patents. See p. 8.

3) The alternative approach to product development is for firms to be **reactive**. A reactive firm markets **imitative** and **replacement products**. Smaller companies usually take this approach, as they have less money to invest in R&D.

New Products need a Unique Selling Point (USP)

Every successful new product, whether it be innovative, imitative or a replacement for an existing product, needs to have something that **differentiates** it from the **competition**. This is known as a **Unique Selling Point** or a **Unique Selling Proposition (USP)**.

1) Products have **tangible benefits** and **intangible benefits**. Both can be used as USPs.

2) **Tangible benefits** can be **measured**. Products with tangible benefits that could be used as USPs are things like low-calorie pizza, energy-efficient fridges and savings accounts with high rates of interest.

3) **Intangible benefits** are things that can't be measured. They are based on concepts such as reputation and product image. E.g. Beauty products market themselves as making the consumer feel good, certain makes of car are perceived as being reliable, and some fashion brands are seen as 'cool.'

Jim had read the whole manual, but he still couldn't find his computer's USP.

4) A product's tangible and intangible benefits are important, but there are other things the consumer considers. These might be things like **customer service**, **money-back guarantees**, and availability of **spare parts**.

Marketing Mix: Product

New Product Development includes Several Stages

1) **Ideas stage** — Market researchers look for a **gap in the market**, and figure out how a new product can best meet customer needs. The business does **research and development** (R&D) and analyses **competitor** products.

2) **Screening stage** — The business analyses the idea for the new product to see if it's **easy to market**, and to see if it'll make a **profit**. Market researchers find out what **consumers think** about the potential new product. A **prototype** (model) might be made to find out what the new product will really look like in real life.

The relative importance of formal and functional design depends on the product and the market.

3) **Product development stage** — The prototype is turned into a saleable product. The **functional design** of the product (its **structure** and how it **works**) and the **formal design** (its **appearance**) are tuned up and made as good as possible.

4) **Value analysis** — The business tries to make the product good **value** for money. They look at the economy of **making**, **warehousing** and **distributing** the product to make sure the whole process will be **efficient** and give value for money — for the **business** and for the **consumer**.

5) **Testing** — Just before launch, the product may be tested. A small batch of **pilot products** are made, and market research investigates **customer reactions** to them. If the public like it, the **production line** is tooled up to make the product. All systems are go — the business **launches** the product.

Most new products Fail — it's better to fail Sooner rather than Later

New product development is **expensive**. **Limited money** often puts the brakes on development. Sometimes it turns out that the product is **too expensive** to make and wouldn't be profitable.

Products that survive long enough to reach the market can create **new problems** over time:

1) **Fixed-asset** purchases often increase, because companies need new machines, factories etc. to produce the new product.

2) **Revenue expenditure** also tends to increase — the company needs to purchase materials to make the new product, and if it needs to employ extra staff, it has to pay their wages, too. This all affects the company's **liquidity** (the amount of cash it has available to use).

3) It can be difficult for firms to create **customer confidence and loyalty**. Lots of customers will buy a new product once, but it can be hard to get them to make repeat purchases. This is especially true for firms which are still young.

In the first few months of their life, the business spends much more on new products than they bring in in revenue This tends to even out over time.

Practice Questions

Q1 There are three types of new product. What are they called?

Q2 What is the benefit for a company of having a product with a unique selling point?

Q3 What are the stages of new product development?

Exam Questions

Q1 Explain why a small company which is new to the market might prefer to launch an imitative, rather than innovative, product.

(4 marks)

Q2 Sam and Bob want to open a luxury chocolate shop, and want to make sure their product is unique. Explain what is meant by a USP and give four examples of USPs they could use for their product.

(5 marks)

Most new products fail — sounds like they could do with a revision guide...

Launching a product sounds easy — if you can't come up with your own idea, you can just imitate someone else or replace something that exists already. It's tougher than it looks though, which means that, of all the crazy new product ideas that people come up with every day, only a tiny proportion ever live to see the shelves...it's quite a sad story really.

Marketing Mix: Product

All products are born with no sales at all. If they're looked after, they grow into big strong products with lots of sales, then they get married and have lots of spin-offs ... er, maybe.

Products *have a* Life Cycle

The product life cycle shows the **sales** of a product over **time**.

It's useful for planning **marketing strategies** and changing the **marketing mix**.

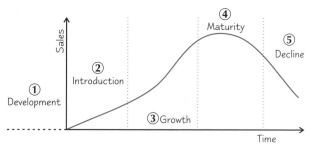

1 — Development

1) The **research and development** (R&D) department **develop** the product.
2) The **marketing** department does **market research**.
3) The **costs** are **high**, and there aren't any sales yet to cover the costs.
4) Development has a **high failure rate**. This is because there's often **not enough demand**, or because the business can't make the product **cheaply** enough to make a profit.

2 — Introduction

1) The product is **launched**, either in one market or in several markets. It's sometimes launched with **complementary** products — e.g. the PlayStation® was launched with games.
2) The business often **promotes** the product heavily to build sales — but businesses need to make sure they've got enough **resources** and **capacity** to **meet the demand** that promotions create.
3) The **initial price** of the product may be **high** to cover **promotional costs**. This is called **skimming** (see p.67).
4) Alternatively, the price can start off **low** to encourage sales. This is **penetration pricing** (see p.67).
5) Sales go up, but the sales revenue has to pay for the high **fixed cost** of development **before** the product can make a **profit**. The business usually ditches products with disappointing sales after this stage.
6) There aren't many **outlets** for the new product.
7) Competition may be **limited** (if it's an **innovative** product).

3 — Growth

1) Sales grow fast. There are **new customers** and **repeat** customers.
2) **Economies of scale** mean the price of manufacturing a unit goes down the more you make, so **profits rise**.
3) **Competitors** may be attracted to the market. Promotion shows **differences** from the competitors' products.
4) The product is often **improved** or **developed**.
5) Rising sales encourage **more outlets** to stock the product.

4 — Maturity

1) **Sales** reach a **peak** and profitability increases because **fixed costs** of **development** have been **paid for**.
2) At **saturation** (when the market is full and has reached maximum growth) sales may begin to drop, depending on the product. Sales are more likely to drop for long-lasting products that customers do not need to replace regularly. The price is often reduced to stimulate **demand**, which reduces profits.
3) There aren't many new customers. **Competition** within the industry becomes fierce — again sales might **suffer**.

5 — Decline

1) The product doesn't **appeal** to customers any more. **Sales fall** rapidly and profits decrease.
2) On the other hand, the product may just stay profitable if **promotional costs** are **low** enough.
3) If sales carry on falling, the product is **withdrawn** or **sold** to another business (selling a product to another company is called **divestment**).

Marketing Mix: Product

Extension Strategies keep a product Going Strong for Longer

Extension strategies try to prolong the life of the product by changing the **marketing mix**. They include:

1) **Product development** — businesses **improve**, reformulate or **redesign** a product. They can change the design of **packaging** to make it look more up to date, or make **special editions** of the product. This can also give a **new focus** to existing **marketing** campaigns.

2) **Market development** — businesses can find **new markets** or **new uses** for existing products, for example by aiming a product at a new market **segment** (e.g. selling baby oil and baby powder for adult use).

3) A business can change the way the product's **distributed** — by selling through the **internet**, selling through **supermarkets** or convenience stores, etc.

4) A business can change the way the product's **priced**.

5) A business can change the way they **promote** the product — by running a new **ad campaign**, for example.

Decline isn't inevitable — it's usually caused by products becoming obsolete, changing consumer tastes or poor marketing. Quality products with excellent original design (e.g. Cadbury's Dairy Milk) can carry on selling for **decades**.

Cash Flow Depends on the Product Life Cycle stage

Cash flow is the difference between **money coming in** and **money going out**. Money comes in from **outside investment** (especially at the start of the life cycle) and from **sales** (mostly later on). Money goes out as **fixed** and **variable costs**. If more money comes in than goes out, cash flow is **positive**. If more goes out than comes in, cash flow is **negative**.

1) At the **development** stage, cash flow is likely to be **negative**. Money is being spent on research and development and there aren't any sales to cover costs.

2) At **introduction**, cash flow is still **negative**. The product is likely to have **cost more** than it makes in sales.

3) As the product goes into the **growth** phase, **cash flow perks up**. Promotion costs should go down, and at the same time sales should be increasing.

4) When the product is in the **maturity** phase, cash flow is **positive**. Sales are **high** and unit **costs** are **low**.

5) In the **decline** phase, sales fall and this might lead to cash flow becoming **negative** again.

The Product Life Cycle stage affects Capacity Utilisation

1) **Capacity** is the **maximum amount** of a product that a business can produce at a particular point in time.

2) **Capacity utilisation** is **how much** of the capacity a business is using.

3) Before a business launches a product, it has to work out how many it'll need to make to fulfil **demand** at the **peak** of the life cycle. It should have those **production resources** in place at the **beginning** of the product life cycle — it's less upheaval than installing new production line machinery every few weeks to keep up with demand.

4) **Capacity utilisation** at **introduction** is **low**. See p.46-47 for more on capacity utilisation

Practice Questions

Q1 What are the stages of the product life cycle?

Q2 What are extension strategies?

Q3 What happens to cash flow during the growth stage of a product's life cycle?

Q4 Why does profitability increase in the maturity phase of the product life cycle?

Exam Questions

Q1	Describe what happens to cash flow during a product's life cycle.	(5 marks)
Q2	To what extent are declining sales inevitable for products?	(10 marks)

No product can live for ever — except maybe the wheel...

There's a lot to learn on these pages, I'll give you that. If you take it step by step, it's fairly straightforward though — it really just goes through the different stages in the life cycle of a product. And if you know the product life cycle inside out, it won't be so hard to learn the other bits mentioned here about extension strategies, cash flows and capacity utilisation.

Marketing Mix: Promotion

Promotion — basically it means using advertising, branding, sales promotion and PR to sell more products.

Promotion *is part of the* Marketing Mix

1) Promotion is designed either to **inform** customers about a product or service, or to **persuade** them to buy it.

2) **Promotional objectives** include increasing **sales** and **profits**, and increasing **awareness** of the product.

3) All promotion has to get the customer's **attention** so that they can be informed or persuaded about the product.

Many companies choose to Advertise *through the* Media

1) Advertising is **non-personal communication** from a business to the public.

2) Ads are used to **promote goods and services** — and also to promote a firm's **public image**.

3) Advertising uses various **media** including print, film, TV, radio, billboards (also called hoardings) and the internet. There are adverts on buses, on bus stops, on the pavement — almost **everywhere**.

4) The choice of media depends partly on the **number of target customers** and the number of **readers** or **viewers** who'll **see** the ad. Ideally, a business wants its adverts to be seen by as **much** of the target market as possible.

5) Advertising **costs** a business **money**. The cost of an advertising campaign must be **worth it** in terms of the **extra sales** it creates. TV adverts at prime viewing times are very expensive. Ads shown when fewer people are watching are cheaper, but have less impact, as they don't reach as many people.

6) The **impact** of an ad is very important. Just as the impact of a TV ad varies depending on what time it is shown, the impacts of ads in other types of media vary too. An advert that covers a two-page spread in a magazine has much more impact that a single page, or a small ad stuck in the classified section at the back.

7) **Specialist media** are used to advertise specialist products to **niche markets**. For example, a manufacturer of fish hooks would do better to advertise in a monthly fishing magazine than in the Daily Telegraph newspaper.

8) **Mass media** are mainly used to advertise **mass market consumer** products and services. However, **business** equipment like computer systems and stationery are advertised on **TV** these days, so it's not right to say that mass media advertising is **only** for consumer products.

9) There are **legal constraints** on advertising some products. E.g. companies are not allowed to suggest that alcohol can make people socially or sexually successful. Cigarette advertising is banned altogether.

10) The **Advertising Standards Agency (ASA)** regulates advertising in the UK. It makes sure that advertisements **do not mislead**, do not cause **serious or widespread offence** or **harm**, are **socially responsible** and have regard for **fair competition**.

The TV remote — scourge of TV advertisers everywhere. People are changing channel when the ads come on, the FIENDS...

Advertising *changes during a* Product Life Cycle

See p.62-63 for more on product life cycles.

1) Products are often heavily advertised at **launch**. If a product is completely **new** to the market, the adverts are **informative**. They tell customers about the product.

2) During the **growth** phase, advertising **differentiates** between brands. It persuades consumers that the product is different from and better than the competitor products. The objective of advertising in the growth phase is to **maintain** or **increase market share**.

3) When a product is at the **mature, saturation** phase, consumers need to be **reminded** of it. If the manufacturer has an **extension** strategy, they can use advertising to inform consumers about, say, any **improvements** they've made to their product.

Branding *is a key aspect of* Product Image

Branding can be very useful when it comes to advertising — not only does it give a product an identity, but it differentiates it from the competition.

1) **Homogenous** (generic) products are the same no matter which business sells them. Brands are **unique**.

2) Brands are important because customers pay a **premium price** for them, and customers are **loyal** to them. Brands have a specific **brand image** — a good brand has a lot of **intangible benefits** for the customer.

3) Brands can be **individual** products — like Sprite® or Daz or KitKat®. They can also be "family brands" which cover a **range** of products, like Heinz or NIKE.

4) Packaging is important because it helps to **distinguish** the product, e.g. the Coca-Cola® bottle. Packaging also helps to give a good **image** of a product. Packaging isn't important for all products though, e.g. those in industrial markets. A box of **fancy chocolates** needs attractive packaging, but a bulk order of **printer toner** doesn't.

Marketing Mix: Promotion

Not All promotion involves Advertising

1) Manufacturers often offer **sales promotions**. These are things like **special offers**, e.g. "buy one get one free" (**BOGOF**), competitions, free gifts, **sponsorship** and **trade-ins**. Sales promotions can be aimed straight at the **customer** to **raise awareness** or **increase sales** of a product. Manufacturers also aim sales promotions at the **retailer** to encourage them to **stock** more of their products.

2) **Merchandising** means ensuring that retailers are displaying a company's products as effectively as possible. Some merchandisers offer retailers **point of sale displays** (e.g. special colourful racks with the company logo).

3) **Direct mail** means **mailshots** sent out to customers. The customer usually hasn't **asked** to receive them. Businesses that keep information about their customers on a database can **target** their direct mail to particular consumer groups. Direct mail that is untargeted ("**junk mail**") can sometimes be a **waste of money**, because it often just gets thrown away.

4) **Personal selling** or **direct selling** is personal communication between a **salesperson** and a customer. Personal selling can involve sales assistants in shops as well as travelling salespeople and phone salespeople.

5) **Event sponsorship** makes consumers aware of a firm and its product. It also gives the firm a good image.

6) **Direct Response TV Marketing** encourages consumers to contact the advertiser directly to purchase a product they have seen advertised on television. **Shopping channels** are an example of this kind of promotion.

PR gets Businesses or Products Good Publicity in the Media

Public relations (PR) is a key form of promotion. Many companies have **specialist PR departments**.
1) PR involves **liaising** with the **media**, writing **press releases**, and answering **enquiries** from the press.
2) PR departments write **brochures**, **newsletters** and **leaflets** giving information about the company.
3) Public relations deals with things like **product launches**, **conferences** and other **special events**.

The Promotional Mix reflects Product, Budget and Competitor Activity

1) Businesses use a **mixture** of methods to promote products. The combination of promotional techniques that a business uses to promote a product is called the **promotional mix**. The main elements in the mix are often **personal selling** and **advertising**. Other methods have a supporting role.

2) The promotional mix depends on: the **product** itself, the **market**, **competitor activity**, the **product life cycle** (see p.62-63) and the **budget** available.

3) In general, **inexpensive**, **simple** products purchased by the **consumer** are promoted by **advertising**.

4) **Expensive** and **complex** products are more likely to be promoted by **personal selling**. So are products or services sold in the **industrial market**.

5) **Consumer durables**, for example **cars** or **washing machines**, are often sold by a combination of **advertising** and **personal selling**. TV, print and billboard adverts **attract the buyer** into the showroom, where the salesperson moves in for the kill.

6) Manufacturers use different methods to sell their product to a **retailer** than to sell it to the **final customer**. Businesses often use **salespeople** to get **shops** to stock their product, and **advertising** to persuade **customers** to buy the product in the shops.

Practice Questions

Q1 What two things is promotion designed to do?
Q2 In which phase of the product life cycle does advertising stress differences with competitor products?
Q3 What is meant by "PR"?

Exam Questions

Q1 Discuss how a business might change its advertising according to a product's position in its life cycle. (4 marks)

Q2 Analyse how a manufacturer of breakfast cereal could promote its product, if it did not want to advertise. (10 marks)

We want people to buy our product — that's why we tell them to BOGOF...

When it comes to promotion, it's all in the mix. You'll need to suggest which combination of methods would best suit a firm, and why. It's important to consider budget too — most companies can't afford to have David Beckham in their ads.

Marketing Mix: Price

The basics rules of pricing are obvious — a firm needs to price its product so that it covers its costs but is still affordable for the consumer. Products often change price at different stages in their life cycle.

Pricing **Strategy** is a **Long-term** plan — **Tactics** only work in the **Short-term**

1) Pricing **strategies** are the way in which a company plans to price a product for the **medium** to **long-term** future.
2) Price **skimming** and **penetration** pricing are both pricing **strategies**.
3) Price **tactics** are **short-term** measures which are introduced in response to particular **issues** or **problems**.
4) **Loss leaders** and **psychological pricing** are two types of **tactics** companies often use.

Price Discrimination means charging **Different Customers Different Prices**

When a company sells its product at different prices to different groups of consumers, this is called **price discrimination**.

1) Price discrimination often occurs when consumers are **buying a service in advance**. Hotel rooms, air travel and rail tickets are all examples of this. Prices change as the **departure date gets nearer**. They can also change according to the **day** or **time** that a customer wants to travel.

2) Other companies might vary prices according to the **age** or **social status** of their customers. **Theatres**, **cinemas** and **theme parks** sell tickets at different rates to **OAPs**, **students**, **under-16s** and **families**.

Cheap theatre tickets — one reason why it's great to be old.

3) The advantage of price discrimination is that it allows companies to **respond quickly to changes in demand**. If demand is high at a particular time, prices rise, and if demand is low, prices go down. It also allows firms to offset some of the costs of having **excess capacity**.

4) Companies need to make sure it's possible to **separate out the different markets** before using price discrimination. Building merchants, e.g. Ridgeons, sell to businesses at lower prices, so they need to be able to tell the difference between their trade and private customers. Otherwise they might sell to private customers at trade prices by mistake.

Existing Products can be either **Price Leaders** or **Takers**

Strategies for existing products:

1) A **price leader** is an existing brand that's in such a **powerful position** within the market that it sets the price, and other businesses follow. Rival businesses know that consumers see the price leader as **the** brand of tea bags or baked beans, so they'll have to price their own rival product a tiny bit lower or nobody will buy it.
2) **Competition** reduces prices. In very competitive markets, **buyers dictate the price**, and sellers have to **take whatever price** the buyer is willing to pay — this is called **price taking**. E.g. milk producers selling to supermarkets are **price takers**.
3) **Predatory pricing** is when a business **deliberately lowers prices** to force another business **out of the market** — e.g. a large nationwide company might target a successful but small local competitor by lowering their prices in that area until the small competitor **goes out of business**. Prices can stay high in all other areas, so the business will lose little money overall, and once the competitor has gone they will **raise** their prices again.
4) **Competitive pricing** is when companies **monitor** their **competitors' prices** to make sure that their own prices are set at an equal or lower level. **Supermarkets** and **department stores** often use this method. Some stores will **refund the difference** in price if you are able to find a product cheaper somewhere else.

Marketing Mix: Price

Psychological Pricing and Loss Leaders help to attract More Customers

Businesses use certain **tactics** to ensure they make profitable sales. For example:

1) **Psychological pricing** bases the price on customers' **expectations** about what to pay.
For instance, a high price may make people think the product is high quality,
and £99.99 seems better than £100 even though it's only 1p difference.

2) **Loss leaders** are products sold at or below cost price. These products may well **lose money**, but the idea is that
they'll make a profit for the business indirectly anyway, e.g. by enticing customers into the shop where they'll
probably buy full-priced items too. The loss leaders can be widely advertised to encourage this. This tactic can
work well in **supermarkets**, where customers will usually buy lots of other items as well as the loss leader.

Companies use Promotional Pricing Strategies when launching New Products

1) **New and innovative products** are often sold at **high prices** when they first reach the market. This is known as
skimming, or **creaming**. Consumers will pay more because the product has **scarcity value**, and the high price
boosts the **product's image** and increases its appeal. New **technological products**, such as computers,
tend to be priced using this method. Prices are then dropped quite considerably when the product
has been on the market for a year or so.

2) **Skimming** is a good strategy to use if a company can **protect its product** to make sure competitors
don't launch an imitative product at a lower price. They might use **patents** or **trademarks**
to stop other people copying their idea.

3) **Penetration pricing** is the opposite of skimming. It means launching a product at a **low price** in order to
attract customers and gain **market share**. It is especially effective in markets which are **price-sensitive**.

4) **Penetration pricing** works best for companies that can benefit from **economies of scale**
(e.g. lower costs) when manufacturing large quantities of a product.

Several Factors affect Demand for a product

1) The **price of the product** affects demand. As the price goes up, demand
tends to go down. As the price goes down, demand goes up.

2) The **price of similar products** affects demand. When one manufacturer
increases its prices, demand for **cheaper competitor products** tends to **rise**.

3) **Customer income** affects demand. When people have **more money to spend**, there's
more demand.

4) **Seasonality** affects demand. E.g. the demand for soft drinks is greater in the **summer**.

5) Successful **marketing** stimulates demand.

No one was sure which was falling faster — Jim, or demand for tiny swimming trunks.

Practice Questions

Q1   What is meant by "pricing strategy"?

Q2   What is the difference between a price leader and a price taker?

Q3   What kind of products tend to be sold using the skimming method?

Q4   Give three examples of factors other than price which affect demand.

Exam Questions

Q1   Analyse why a hotel might benefit from pricing its rooms according
to a strategy of price discrimination.   (6 marks)

Q2   A small company is launching a new brand of fruit juice. Suggest which pricing methods it should
consider, and explain why.   (6 marks)

Skimming and creaming — both ways of milking profits...

*When it comes to pricing, most companies use a cost-based method and throw in the occasional bit of promotional
pricing to keep consumers interested. The key point to remember is that price isn't the only thing that bothers customers
— a lot of people would rather buy high quality chicken nuggets than cheap ones made of scrawny bits of chicken neck.*

Marketing Mix: Price

OK, so price isn't the only thing that affects demand, but it can certainly have a pretty major impact. Just how big or small that impact is depends on the price elasticity of demand.

Price Elasticity of Demand shows how Demand changes with Price

1) **Price elastic** products have a **large percentage change in demand** for a **small percentage change in price**.

2) **Price <u>inelastic</u>** products are the opposite — there's a **small percentage change in demand** for a **big percentage change in price**.

$$\text{Price elasticity of demand} = \frac{\text{\% change in quantity demanded}}{\text{\% change in price}}$$

They won't ask you to do this calculation in the exam. They'll give you the elasticity coefficient and you'll just need to use it to say how price change affects revenue.

Example: A price **rise** of **10%** results in a **30% reduction** in demand.

$$\text{Price elasticity of demand} = \frac{-30\%}{+10\%} = -3$$

Price **elastic**, because the price elasticity of demand is **more than 1** (ignoring the minus sign).

Basically, as price goes up demand falls, and vice versa.

Example: A price **reduction** of **20%** results in a **5% increase** in demand.

$$\text{Price elasticity of demand} = \frac{+5\%}{-20\%} = -0.25$$

This is called the elasticity coefficient.

Price **inelastic**, because the price elasticity of demand is **less than 1**.

3) Price elasticity of demand is **always negative**, so ignore the minus sign. This is because a positive change in price causes a negative change in demand, and a negative change in price causes a positive change in demand.

4) If the price elasticity of demand is **greater than 1** (ignoring the minus sign), the product is **price elastic**. If the price elasticity of demand is **less than 1**, it's **price inelastic**. So, −3 is price elastic and −0.25 is price inelastic.

Price Elasticity affects Revenue and Profit

1) **Sales revenue = price** of product × **quantity sold**. Price elasticity shows how price affects sales revenue.

2) If demand is **price elastic**, a **price increase** will make **sales revenue go down**. The **% decrease in sales** will be **more** than the **% increase in price**.

3) If demand is price **inelastic**, a rise in **price** will make **sales revenue go up**. The % decrease in sales isn't big enough to offset the % increase in price.

4) If demand is **price elastic**, a firm can **increase revenue** by reducing price, which then greatly increases the number of sales. **But profit = revenue − cost**, and more sales often mean **higher costs**. The **profits** will only increase if the **rise in revenue** is **more** than the **rise in costs**.

5) If demand is **price inelastic**, **decreasing** the **price** will make **sales increase** slightly. Sales **revenue goes down** because the price has fallen and only a few more units have been sold.

Price change	PED more than 1 (elastic)	PED equal to 1	PED less than 1 (inelastic)
Increase in price	Sales revenue decreases	Sales revenue doesn't change	Sales revenue increases
Decrease in price	Sales revenue increases	Sales revenue doesn't change	Sales revenue decreases

This table shows how price changes affect sales revenue.

Example: A company makes scarves and sells them for £11. Annual sales are 9600 scarves. The product's elasticity coefficient is −2.5. If they increase the price to £12.10, calculate the change in revenue.

Current revenue: £11 × 9600 = £105 600

% change in quantity demanded: 10% change in price × 2.5 elasticity coefficient = 25% decrease

25% of 9600: 9600 × 0.25 = 2400 **New sales:** 9600 − 2400 = 7200 **New revenue** = 7200 × £12.10 = £87 120

Change in revenue: £105 600 − £87 120 = £18 480 decrease in revenue

It can be Hard to Work Out price elasticity of demand

1) Estimating price elasticity of demand is **difficult** because price isn't the **only** factor affecting demand. An increase in demand for ice cream could be partly down to **hot weather** and/or a good **advertising** campaign.

2) Businesses use **primary market research** (see p.12) to ask people if they'd buy a product for a **higher** or **lower price**. This can give a good idea of the relationship between **price** and **demand**.

3) However, the values used in price elasticity calculations may be wrong. The calculations are often based on **estimates** of percentage change in price and demand, or on **unrepresentative** data. The market may have **changed** since the data was collected and the market research itself may be unreliable or inaccurate.

Marketing Mix: Price

Price elasticity of demand Depends on Ease of Switching Brands

1) If a consumer can **easily switch** to a **competitor** product, the demand will be **price elastic**. This will result in customers jumping ship and buying the **competitor's product** instead.

2) Businesses try to **differentiate** their products to create **brand loyalty**. **Loyal** customers won't switch even if the price goes up, so this makes the demand **less** price elastic.

3) It's easier for customers to switch if they can **compare prices** and find cheaper alternatives. The **internet** makes it easier to switch and **increases price elasticity**.

4) People tend not to switch to alternatives in the **short term**. They **take time** to get **fed up** with a product.

5) **Product types** tend to be **price inelastic**, but individual **brands** tend to be **price elastic**. For example, **petrol** sales are **inelastic** because all cars need fuel. The sales of an **individual company's petrol** are **elastic** because motorists can easily go to a **cheaper filling station**.

Income Elasticity of Demand shows how Demand changes with Income

When people earn **more money**, there's **more demand** for some products.
Funnily enough, there's **less demand** for other products.

$$\text{Income elasticity of demand} = \frac{\% \text{ change in quantity demanded}}{\% \text{ change in real incomes}}$$

Example: A **rise** in income of **10%** results in a **5% increase** in demand.

$$\text{Income elasticity of demand} = \frac{+5\%}{+10\%} = +0.5$$

Change in real income means change in income, taking into account how prices have changed (usually increased) over the same period.

1) **Normal goods** have a **positive income elasticity of demand** that's **less than 1**. This means that as **income rises**, the **demand** for normal goods **rises** — but at a **slower rate** than the increase in income.

2) **Luxury goods** have a **positive income elasticity of demand** which is **more than 1**. This means that the **demand for luxury goods** grows **faster** than the increase in income.

3) In a business sense, "**inferior**" goods are cheaper 'value' products — taking a **coach** instead of the **train**, for example, or eating a **cheaper supermarket value brand** of baked beans because you can't afford **Heinz baked beans**. Inferior goods have a **negative income elasticity of demand** — **demand falls** when **income rises** and **demand rises** when **income falls**.

Elasticity helps a business make Choices

1) **Price elasticity** helps a manufacturer **decide** whether to **raise** or **lower** the price of a product. They can see what might happen to the sales, and ultimately what will happen to sales revenue.

2) **Income elasticity** helps a manufacturer see what'll happen to sales if the **economy** grows or shrinks.

Practice Questions

Q1 If a product has an elasticity coefficient of –0.9, is it elastic or inelastic?

Q2 Give two reasons why it can be difficult to calculate price elasticity.

Q3 What kind of products become less popular when there's an increase in income?

Answer on p. 78.

Exam Questions

Q1 A company sells 200 horses a year for £1500 each. If the elasticity coefficient is –0.7, calculate the impact on revenue that a 15% increase in prices will have. (9 marks)

Q2 Explain why product differentiation reduces elasticity of demand. (3 marks)

Rubber prices are usually the most elastic...

The clues are in the names with these two — price elasticity shows how much price influences demand, and income elasticity shows how much demand is affected by income. The method for working out changes in revenue using the elasticity coefficient has quite a few steps, so make sure you get your head round each and every one of them...

Marketing Mix: Place

Distribution is important. This is the "place" part of the marketing mix. If a product can't get to the marketplace, no one can buy it. Needs go unfulfilled, companies don't make profits, anarchy reigns...

It's **Vital** to get the **Product** to the **Consumer**

A **channel** of **distribution** is the route a product takes from the producer to the consumer. A product usually passes through **intermediaries** on the way from producer to consumer — e.g. **retailers**, **wholesalers** and **agents**.

1) **Retailers** are **shops** who sell to consumers. They're usually the **final stage** in the distribution channel. Tesco, Argos and Amazon.co.uk® are **retailers**. Retailers can be physical shops or online "e-tailers".

2) **Wholesalers** buy products cheaply in **bulk** and **sell them on** to **retailers**. Wholesalers make life **easier** for retailers and manufacturers:

   - Wholesalers **buy** goods from manufacturers in bulk and **sell** them in **smaller quantities** to **retailers**. This is called "**breaking bulk**" — a wholesaler takes the goods off the manufacturer's hands and **pays** for the whole lot. Manufacturers don't have to **wait** for customers to buy the goods before they see any cash.

   - Wholesalers make distribution **simpler**. Without a wholesaler, the manufacturer would have to make **separate deliveries** to lots of retailers, and send each and every retailer an **invoice**. Selling to one wholesaler cuts down the paperwork and the number of journeys.

   - Wholesalers can **store more goods** than a retailer can — they act as the retailer's storage cupboard.

3) **Agents** act on behalf of **manufacturers**. See below for more about the role of an agent.

There are **Different Channels** of **Distribution**

Channels of distribution have different levels. It's more expensive, but sometimes necessary, to have a **multi-layered** channel.

In a zero-level channel, a product or service goes straight from producer to consumer.

| Manufacturer | ⟹ | Consumer |

A one-level channel has one intermediary.

| Manufacturer | ⟶ | Retailer | ⟹ | Consumer |

| Manufacturer | ⟹ | Agent | ⟶ | Consumer |

A two-level channel has two intermediaries — usually a wholesaler and retailer.

| Manufacturer | ⟶ | Wholesaler | ⟹ | Retailer | ⟹ | Consumer |

A three-level channel has three intermediaries.

| Manufacturer | ⟹ | Agent | ⟹ | Wholesaler | ⟹ | Retailer | ⟹ | Consumer |

Direct Selling: Manufacturer → Consumer

Accountants, electricians and hairdressers sell their **services** direct to the consumer. The **internet** has made it **easier** for producers of goods to sell **direct** to the consumer. Direct selling is now very popular, and is done through door-to-door sales, TV shopping channels, telephone sales and mail-order catalogues.

Indirect Selling: Manufacturer → Retailer → Consumer

Large supermarkets buy goods in bulk direct from the manufacturer and have them delivered either straight from the manufacturer or via their own warehouses.

Indirect Selling: Manufacturer → Wholesaler → Retailer → Consumer

This is the **traditional** distribution channel used for **fast moving consumer goods** (known as FMCG).

Direct Selling through an agent: Manufacturer → Agent → Consumer

An agent is like a sales representative, except they are not employed by the company whose goods they sell. They get commission (a percentage of the value of the goods they sell) instead of being paid a salary. Ann Summers lingerie is sold by **agents** through **party plans** — people invite friends to their **home** and an **agent** sells the goods **at the party**. Some **mail-order catalogues** (e.g. Avon) use agents who place orders on behalf of other people and collect payments from them.

Retailers often use **Several Channels** of **Distribution**

Many firms now sell goods via the internet. Having an online store can affect the way a company distributes goods.

1) Stores which **only** sell **online** may have **cheaper costs**, because they use a **single** channel of distribution. However they can have **problems** establishing **brand loyalty**.

2) Companies such as supermarkets and fashion retailers which have high street stores as well as an internet store are using a **multi-channel strategy**. This may lead to added costs if they are supplying goods from different warehouses, but it also allows them to target a wider market.

Over a third of the UK population now uses the Internet for shopping.

3) For small firms, a low-cost option is to sell goods using **auction sites** or **electronic marketplaces** (e.g. eBay™).

Marketing Mix: Place

Businesses choose a *Channel* of *Distribution* to *Suit Their Needs*

The choice of distribution channel is a compromise between cost, ease and control.

1) It's **more profitable** to **sell direct** to the customer. Each intermediary (party) in the distribution chain takes a **slice of profit** from the manufacturer — wholesalers and retailers have to make money too. Businesses that **sell direct** can offer their product at a **lower price** than **retailers** at the end of a long distribution chain.

2) On the other hand, it's **easier** to use **intermediaries**. It'd be a hassle to distribute a small amount of product to lots of little shops. It's easier to sell to a **wholesaler** who can deliver products from several manufacturers in a single delivery. Using a wholesaler gives a manufacturer the chance of more **market coverage**.

3) The **fewer intermediaries** in the distribution chain, the more **control** a manufacturer has over how its products are sold. It has more say in the **final selling price** and how the product is **promoted**.

4) UK **retail trends** have **changed** in recent years, as retailers have found **cheaper** or **more effective** ways of distributing their products. **Out-of-town retail parks**, **concessions** (shops within shops), and **mail-order catalogues** have **cheaper overheads** than high street stores and can sometimes offer customers other **benefits**, such as **free parking**. **Factory outlets** allow firms to make a return on **imperfect goods** (seconds) or **last season's stock**.

There are no real hard and fast rules about which distribution channel a business might choose, but there are a few trends.

Short Distribution Channels	Long Distribution Channels
Industrial products	Consumer products
Few customers	Many customers
Customers concentrated in one place	Customers widely spread out
Expensive, complex goods	Inexpensive, simple goods
Infrequent sales	Frequent sales
Bulky products	Small products
Bespoke (made to measure) products	Standard products
Services	Goods

Businesses set **distribution targets**. They might set a target of £X worth of sales through supermarkets, or selling to more retail outlets in a particular area of the country. Businesses can use a number of **different strategies** to **achieve** their distribution targets, e.g. offering discounts to particular retailers, or using advertising in trade magazines.

Different Distribution Strategies *suit different products*

1) **Everyday groceries** and **convenience** items need to be distributed as **widely** as possible. Consumers want to be able to buy things like a newspaper, a pint of milk and a bar of chocolate at a convenient local shop. They don't want to travel 20 miles to a "Pints Of Milk R Us" superstore.

2) **Luxury** goods don't need to be widely distributed. Manufacturers of luxury goods like to sell them in a small number of **exclusive** shops — it's about **quality**, not quantity.

3) Specialist goods like electrical products need to be distributed to **specialist** shops. Consumers like to be able to **compare** several different kinds of computer or CD player before buying, and often need specialist advice and assistance when choosing what to buy.

Practice Questions

Q1 What is the role of a wholesaler?
Q2 Name two types of distribution channel.
Q3 What kind of distribution channel is traditionally used for FMCG?
Q4 What kind of distribution strategy is needed for everyday groceries?

Exam Questions

Q1 Analyse the different factors a firm must consider when deciding on an appropriate channel of distribution. (8 marks)

Q2 Evaluate internet sales as a distribution channel for luxury consumer goods. (7 marks)

I'm a new product — get me out of here...

Distribution can seem like a mundane, boring thing. Yes, it is all about warehouses full of cardboard boxes, fleets of trucks going from A to B and little men popping catalogues through your letterbox. But on the other hand it's a vital part of the wondrous marketing mix. Where you can buy something is a big factor in deciding whether to buy it.

Improving Competitiveness

Competition is good for the consumer, but not so great for businesses. Companies are always trying to improve their competitiveness and steal market share from their competitors — usually by changing their marketing mix.

Competition is Beneficial to the Consumer

Most businesses operate in a **competitive market**. A competitive market is one where there are lots of companies selling products which are roughly the same. As far as the customer is concerned, competition is good news:

1) It forces **prices down**.
2) It tends to **improve** customer **services**.
3) It **improves** the **quality** of goods on offer.

The amount of Competition depends on the Market Conditions

Not all markets are structured in the same way. Some markets have **loads of firms** competing for the same group of consumers, while other markets are made up of just a **few companies**:

1) A **monopoly** is a **market** which has only **one organisation** providing a product or service.

2) The **government** can **intervene** to **stop** companies ending up with a high degree of **monopoly** (i.e. massive market share). This is because a company with a monopoly might **exploit** its **customers** by charging high prices, or **use resources inefficiently**.

3) Nonetheless, **some companies** in the UK do have a **high degree of monopoly**. These include train companies (because there is often only one company operating on each route) and utility companies. The government uses **regulators** to make sure that these companies don't act unfairly.

The Board Game Professors — they've all got high degrees in Monopoly.

4) When there are a few **dominant businesses** in a market, this is called an **oligopoly**. E.g. 4 major supermarket chains dominate the UK groceries market.

5) Other markets consist of **many businesses**, all of whom **know** what **price** the market is charging for a particular product, but are **too small** to **influence** it. This is **perfect competition**. Businesses in this kind of market survive by offering personal and specialist services and attempting to create **niche markets** (see p.8).

The Market Conditions affect the Marketing Mix

1) **Monopolies** have it easy when it comes to the marketing mix — they get to **decide** what **price** they want to charge for their product (within reason) and **don't** really have to worry too much about **marketing**.

2) **Oligopolies** can seem very competitive, as firms operating in this type of market **spend a lot** on their **marketing mix**. However, if one firm cuts prices, all the others usually will too, which means they tend to **compete** on things other than price, such as **special offers** or **advertising**.

3) Where there's **perfect competition**, companies have to **accept** the **price** set by the market. **Marketing isn't** really **possible**, so companies have to be efficient and keep **costs low**.

It's Hard for New Companies to enter the Market

Firms which have a lot of financial and marketing power can create **barriers to entry**. These are **obstacles** which make it **hard** for **new businesses** to **establish themselves** in the market.

1) Creating **high consumer loyalty** means **customers** are **unlikely** to **switch** to a new product which has just entered the market. Businesses establish customer loyalty by **investing** heavily in **advertising** and **branding** (see p.64).

2) **High set-up costs** (such as the cost of **machinery** or **premises**) can also deter new firms from trying to enter the marketplace. This is because they would have to raise very **high** levels of **investment** in order to fund the start-up and they know that they **won't** be able to **recover** this **investment** if they're not successful and choose/are forced to leave the market. Industries with high set-up costs include aviation (airlines) and pharmaceuticals (medicines).

Improving Competitiveness

Changing the Marketing Mix can help to make a business More Competitive

Markets are **dynamic**. This means they are **constantly changing**. New competitors enter the market and failed ones leave, new improved products and services are introduced and aggressive marketing ploys are used.

1) In order to **remain profitable**, companies need to keep **reviewing** their **marketing mix**, taking into account the actions of competitors and other changes in the marketplace.

2) For a company to stay profitable, it needs to stay **competitive**. A business is competitive if it has something that **customers want** or **need** that **other** similar **businesses don't** have.

3) A company can **improve** its **competitiveness** by **changing** any one of the four elements in the **marketing mix**. They can improve the **quality** of the **product**, reassess their methods of **promotion**, use new **pricing strategies**, and reconsider channels of distribution.

4) Having a **unique product** is a key weapon in beating off the competition. Companies invest heavily in **branding** and **design** and protect their products with **patents** to keep the competitors at bay. See p.8 for more on patents.

To find out more about USPs, see p.60.

5) **Technological advances** are another reason why companies might change the mix. Widespread **internet** access has meant that many firms have **changed** their **method of distribution**.

Not all ways of improving Competitiveness involve Marketing

Changing the marketing mix is not the only way of improving competitiveness. Firms can **improve** their **profitability** by **reducing costs**, or they can improve the **quality** of their **service**.

1) Many firms attempt to increase competitiveness by **reducing** their **fixed costs** (see p.26). They may choose to **rationalise** their staffing (see p.47), as staff costs are often their biggest fixed cost. Other ways of reducing fixed costs include switching to **cheaper utility providers** and **cheaper** sources of **raw materials**. Some firms may also **cut back** on **research** and **development**.

Rob wondered if being naked would improve his chances in the swimming competition.

2) Businesses can also improve their competitiveness by improving the **quality** of their **customer service**. Good customer service increases **consumer loyalty** and also encourages customers to **recommend** the **business** to **other people**. Ways of improving customer service include setting **higher standards** for **recruitment** and **training** (for more on these two, see p.42-43).

Practice Questions

Q1 What is meant by a monopoly?

Q2 What is meant by "perfect competition"?

Q3 Why would high set-up costs dissuade a business from entering a market?

Q4 How can a business use non-marketing methods to improve its competitiveness?

Exam Questions

Q1 A luxury hotel in the Lake District has just discovered that a five-star spa hotel is opening just down the road. Discuss how it could make sure it maintains its current market share once the competitor opens? (8 marks)

Exterminate! Exterminate!

It's a cut-throat existence out there in the business world. Threats exist in every type of market, not just in the highly competitive ones. These challenges force businesses to keep changing and updating their services or products, which is ultimately a good thing for the consumer. It's like that saying — what doesn't kill your business can only make it stronger.

Understanding Statistics

There are loads of statistics involved in running a business, so you need to be able to understand what they all mean.

Businesses produce lots of **Statistics**

1) Businesses have a lot of **figures** — e.g. figures for sales, costs, revenues and profit, and market research data.

2) Businesses often deal with **large numbers** — e.g. profits for a small business could be thousands or tens of thousands of pounds (thousand can be written as "k", so 15k means 15 thousand pounds). Big businesses might have very large numbers for sales or revenue figures — millions (a thousand thousand, or 1 000 000) or even billions (a thousand million, or 1 000 000 000).

Remember that negative numbers can be shown by brackets in cash flow forecasts and variance tables.

3) Businesses need to understand what their figures **mean** so that they know how well the business is **performing**, and can forecast how well it will perform in the **future**. In order to understand the data and be able to use it, they present it in a way that makes it **easy** to understand.

Diagrams make data **Easier** to **Understand**

1) **Pie charts** are used for showing **market share**. Each **1% share** is represented by a **3.6°** section of the pie (because there's 360° in a circle and 360 ÷ 100 = 3.6). Pie charts are **simple to use** and **easy** to **understand**. They can be created quickly using **spreadsheets**.

Pie chart showing market share of brands in the cat food market

"Kittibits"

"Megapets"

"Queen of Sheba"

"Purr"

"Furry Pals"   "Kitty Treats"

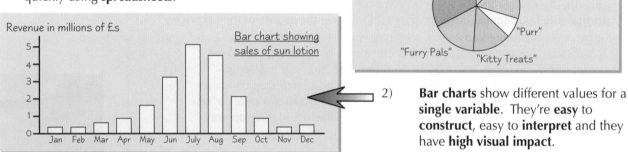

Revenue in millions of £s

Bar chart showing sales of sun lotion

2) **Bar charts** show different values for a **single variable**. They're **easy** to **construct**, easy to **interpret** and they have **high visual impact**.

3) A **histogram** looks quite similar to a bar chart. However, in a histogram the **area** of each block is proportional to the value of the variable measured (not just the height), and there are no gaps between the blocks. So a histogram is different from a bar chart because the bars can vary in both **width** and **height**. Histograms are suitable for comparing variables with **large ranges**.

4) A **pictogram** is a bar chart or histogram where the bars are **pictures** — logos or images. Pictograms are often used in **corporate brochures** — e.g. Cadbury might use pictures of their choccie bars in their sales charts.

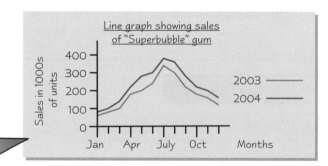

Line graph showing sales of "Superbubble" gum

Sales in 1000s of units

2003
2004

Jan   Apr   July   Oct   Months

5) **Line graphs** plot one variable against another — e.g. sales against time. **More lines** can be added on to show **more variables** — they should be in different colours to keep the graph easy to read.

Diagrams can be **Misleading**

1) Graphs and charts can sometimes give a **false impression** of what is actually going on.

2) If the scales on a graph don't start at **zero**, it can be difficult to see what they show and the meaning can be distorted — e.g. the graph on the right seems to show that the profit has **tripled** between 2004 and 2007, but actually it has only gone up by **10%**.

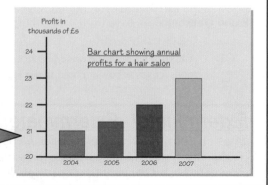

Profit in thousands of £s

Bar chart showing annual profits for a hair salon

Understanding Statistics

You need to be able to *Analyse Data* and *Graphs*

1) As well as being able to read graphs and charts, you need to be able to **analyse** them.

2) This means you need to be able to say what you think is the **important bit** of the chart — e.g. an upward trend in sales, or a big market share.

3) You need to be able to say what you think is **causing** it, and what the potential **effects** might be — e.g. a **decrease** in market share might have been caused by the arrival of a new **competitor**, so the **marketing** budget will have to be **increased** to try to get the market share back.

Data is clustered around an *Average* — *Mean*, *Median* or *Mode*

1) The **mean** is found by **adding together** all numbers in a data set and **dividing** the total by the **number of values** in the data set. Shops often calculate the mean spend per customer as the starting point of a marketing campaign aimed at increasing customers' spending per shop visit.

> Example: 10 customers spend £5.90, £27.98, £13.62, £24.95, £78.81, £16.99, £13.20, £9.95, £2.58 and £14.96.
>
> Mean spend $= \dfrac{5.9 + 27.98 + 13.62 + 24.95 + 78.81 + 16.99 + 13.20 + 9.95 + 2.58 + 14.96}{10} = \dfrac{208.94}{10} = £20.89$

2) The **median** is the **middle** value in a data set once all the values are put in **ascending order** — e.g. a business might rank all salespeople by the revenue they've generated over the past month, then identify the **median** and pay everyone above this position a bonus for good performance.

> Example: 15 sales people generate revenue of £1200, £1350, £1400, £1500, £1600, £1750, £1900, £1950, £2100, £2200, £2340, £2400, £2450, £2500 and £2950.
>
> Median sales revenue = the middle number, which is the 8th number = £1950

3) The **mode** is the **most common number** in a data set. Marks & Spencer might check the modal dress size when planning their shop displays so that the mannequins would reflect the most common body size among British women.

Extensive market research had gone into finding the perfect mannequin to represent today's average British woman.

> Example: 15 women have the following dress sizes:
> 10, 12, 16, 14, 12, 14, 8, 18, 16, 14, 12, 14, 10, 14, 16.
>
> Modal dress size = 14

Obviously M&S would need a much bigger sample than this.

The *Range* of *Data* is *Important* as well

1) **Range** means the **difference** between the **largest** and the **smallest** in a group of numbers.

2) Averages can be a bit misleading. The **mean** of a **small range** of values is likely to give a **true picture** of the data, but the **mean** of a **large** range of values would give a number somewhere in the middle of the range — this wouldn't show that some of the values were actually really big or really small.

3) A **standard deviation** shows the **spread** of a set of values around the average. You don't have to know how to work out a standard deviation. All you need to know is that a **large** standard deviation means the numbers in the original data set are **spread out**, and a **small** standard deviation means they're **clumped close together**.

4) A **confidence level** is another statistical trick. It indicates how **accurate** a conclusion is likely to be. A confidence level of 95% means managers can assume the prediction would be correct 19 times out of 20.

Understanding Statistics

Businesses work out **Percentage Changes** in figures

1) Businesses work out **percentage** increases or decreases in figures like sales volumes, revenue, profit and market share in order to see how performance is **progressing** over time. By looking at percentage changes over a number of months or years, they can see **trends** in the business' performance.

2) The **formula** for working out percentage change is:

$$\text{Percentage change} = \frac{\text{new figure} - \text{previous figure}}{\text{previous figure}} \times 100\%$$

E.g. if sales of umbrellas have gone up from 9 000 to 11 000, the percentage increase in sales is (11 000 – 9 000) ÷ 9 000 × 100% = 22.2%.

3) It's important not to underestimate large changes in figures even if they only produce a small percentage change — e.g. an increase in revenue of £2 million shouldn't be overlooked even if it's only a 3% increase.

Index Numbers show **Changes** in data over time

1) **Index numbers** are a simple way of showing percentage changes in a set of data over time.

2) Businesses take a set of data showing revenue/ profits etc. over a number of years, and make the earliest year the **base year** — the value for the base year is set as 100, and the figures for the following years are shown relative to this figure. E.g. the table below shows the index numbers for revenue for an Italian restaurant:

Year	Total Revenue	Revenue Index (2003 = 100)
2003	£17 000	100
2004	£19 550	115
2005	£21 250	125
2006	£22 440	132
2007	£24 650	145

To work out the revenue index for any year, take the total revenue from that year, divide it by the total revenue in the base year and multiply it by 100, e.g. for 2006:

$$\frac{22\,440}{17\,000} \times 100 = 132$$

3) The main advantage of indexing is that it makes it easy to see trends within the business.

Businesses **Forecast** what **Future** data will be

1) Businessses use data from the past to predict how the business will perform in the future — e.g. if revenue has been going up by around 5% a year for eight years, they might forecast a 5% rise for the coming year.

2) Forecast figures are only estimates though — many factors inside and outside the business might influence how it performs, so it's impossible to be certain that the forecast will be accurate.

Practice Questions

Q1 Why can graphs and charts sometimes be misleading?
Q2 Explain the difference between the "mean", "median" and "mode" of a set of data.
Q3 What do index numbers show?

Exam Questions

Q1	Discuss how statistics can hinder as well as help decision-making.	(10 marks)
Q2	Explain what is meant by "confidence level."	(2 marks)

There are lies, damned lies and statistics...

Statistics can be very helpful but they can also be biased. If you're given a table or graph as part of an exam question, watch out for things like how the axes are labelled, whether the axes start at zero, and whether important info is left out. Remember that businesses often use graphs and charts to put their facts and figures in as good a light as possible.

Answers to Numerical Questions

Section One — Starting a Business

Page 11 — Understanding Markets

Practice Questions

Q2   Market share = sales ÷ total market size × 100%
   = 30 000 ÷ 150 000 × 100% = 20%

Section Two — Financial Planning

Page 27 — Costs, Revenues and Profits

Exam Questions

Q2   (a)   *Maximum of 6 marks available*
   [1 mark for each correct start/finish point of each line]

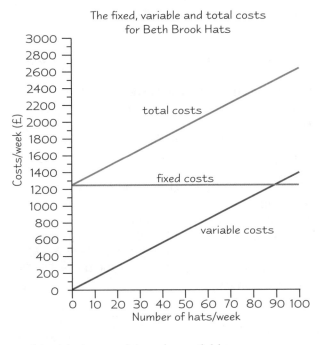

The fixed, variable and total costs for Beth Brook Hats

   (b)   *Maximum of 4 marks available.*
   Costs at 60 hats per week = fixed costs + variable costs **[1 mark]**
   = 1260 + (60 × 14) = £1260 + £840 = £2100 **[1 mark]**
   Revenue = selling price × quantity sold
   = £50 × 60 = £3000   **[1 mark]**
   Profit = revenue – costs = £3000 – £2100 = £900 **[1 mark]**

Page 29 — Break-Even Analysis

Exam Questions

Q2   *Maximum of 4 marks available.*
   Contribution per unit =
   selling price per unit– variable costs per unit **[1 mark]**
   = £13 – £5 = £8 **[1 mark]**
   Break-even point =
   fixed costs ÷ contribution per unit **[1 mark]**
   = £1000 ÷ 8 = 125 customers **[1 mark]**

Page 31 — Cash Flow Forecasting

Practice Questions

Q3   Net cash flow = total cash in – total costs
   = £8000 – £9500 = (£1500)

Q4   Closing balance = opening balance + net cash flow
   = £20 000 + (£7000) = £13 000

Page 33 — Setting Budgets

Practice Questions

Q2   Profit budget = income budget – expenditure budget
   Expenditure budget = income budget – profit budget
   = £125 000 – £30 000 = £95 000

Page 35 — Variances

Practice Questions

Q2   Variance = £15 000 – £18 000 = (£3000)
   so there is a £3000 adverse variance

Exam Questions

Q1   (a)   *Maximum of 10 marks available*

	Feb cumulative variance	Mar budget	Mar actual	Mar variance	Mar cumulative variance
Revenue	£10k (A)	£110k	£120k	£10k (F)	£0
Wages	£9k (F)	£40k	£39k	£1k (F)	£10k (F)
Rent	£1k (A)	£10k	£11k	£1k (A)	£2k (A)
Other costs	£2k (A)	£5k	£5k	£0	£2k (A)
Total costs	£6k (F)	£55k	£55k	£0	£6k (F)

Answers to Numerical Questions

Page 37 — Measuring and Increasing Profit

Practice Questions

Q1 Percentage change in profit
= (current profit – previous profit)
÷ previous profit × 100%
= (£52 000 – £50 000)
÷ £50 000 × 100% = 4%

Exam Questions

Q1 Maximum of 2 marks available.
ROCE = net profit ÷ capital employed × 100% **[1 mark]**
= £100 000 ÷ £40 000 × 100% = 250% **[1 mark]**

Q2 (a) Maximum of 4 marks available.
Net profit = gross profit – fixed costs **[1 mark]**
= £750 000 – £250 000 = £500 000 **[1 mark]**
Net profit margin = net profit ÷ revenue × 100%
[1 mark]
= £500 000 ÷ £2 000 000 × 100%
= 25% **[1 mark]**

Section Three — People in Business

Page 41 — Measuring Workforce Effectiveness

Practice Questions

Q2 Absenteeism
= Number of staff days lost ÷ number of working days
× 100%
Number of working days = number of days company
operates × number of staff – staff holidays
= 245 × 56 – (25 x 56)
= 12320
Absenteeism = 274 ÷ 12320 × 100% = 2.22%
= 2% (to nearest whole percentage).

Q4 Labour turnover
= Number of staff leaving ÷ average number of staff ×
100%
= 18 ÷ 600 × 100% = 3%

Section Four — Operations Management

Page 47 — Capacity Utilisation

Practice Questions
Q1 Capacity utilisation = output ÷ capacity × 100%
= 42 ÷ 65 × 100% = 65% (to nearest whole
percentage).

Q2 Unit cost = total costs ÷ output
= £1600 ÷ 450 = £3.56

Section Five — Marketing and Competition

Page 69 — Marketing Mix: Price

Exam Questions

Q1 Maximum of 9 marks available.
Sales revenue = price of product × quantity sold
[1 mark]
Sales revenue = £1500 × 200 = £300 000 **[1 mark]**

Percentage change in quantity demanded
= percentage change in price × elasticity coefficient
[1 mark]
= 15% × 0.7 elasticity coefficient = 10.5% decrease
[1 mark].

10.5% of 200 (current sales) = 200 × 10.5 ÷ 100 = 21
[1 mark].
New sales = 200 – 21 = 179 **[1 mark]**.
New price = £1500 × 115 ÷ 100 = £1725 **[1 mark]**.
New revenue = £1725 × 179 = £308 775 **[1 mark]**.
Change in revenue = £308 775 – £300 000 = £8775
increase **[1 mark]**.

Get Marks in Your Exam

These pages are meant to get you familiar with how the exam's set out, so that when you turn up on the day, you'll know exactly what to expect from each paper.

The **AS-Level** is broken down into **Two Exams**

If you know what to expect, there won't be any nasty surprises...

1) The Business Studies AS is made up of **two exams** — Unit 1 and Unit 2.

2) Each exam tests a **different** set of **topics** that you'll have covered during the year. Make sure you revise the right set of topics for each exam.

3) The two exams don't have exactly the same **style** of **questions** — so practise answering the different types of questions that can come up.

Unit 1 *is about* **Starting a Small Business**

Unit 1's made up of two topics — **Starting a Business** and **Financial Planning**. These cover the basic requirements of starting a small business. In the financial planning section you have to do calculations, and understand what they show.

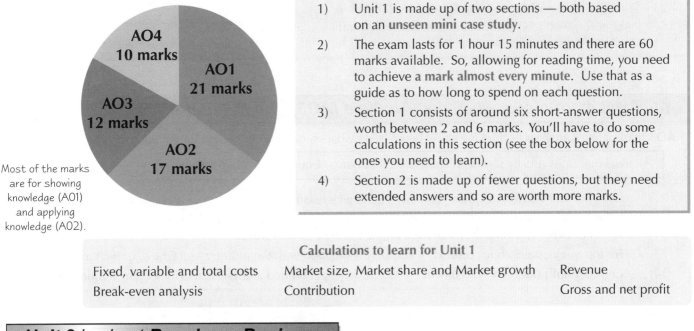

AO4 10 marks
AO1 21 marks
AO3 12 marks
AO2 17 marks

Most of the marks are for showing knowledge (AO1) and applying knowledge (AO2).

1) Unit 1 is made up of two sections — both based on an **unseen mini case study**.

2) The exam lasts for 1 hour 15 minutes and there are 60 marks available. So, allowing for reading time, you need to achieve **a mark almost every minute**. Use that as a guide as to how long to spend on each question.

3) Section 1 consists of around six short-answer questions, worth between 2 and 6 marks. You'll have to do some calculations in this section (see the box below for the ones you need to learn).

4) Section 2 is made up of fewer questions, but they need extended answers and so are worth more marks.

Calculations to learn for Unit 1

Fixed, variable and total costs	Market size, Market share and Market growth	Revenue
Break-even analysis	Contribution	Gross and net profit

Unit 2 *is about* **Running a Business**

Unit 2 has four main sections — **Finance**, **People in Business**, **Operations Management** and **Marketing and Competition**. Although its focus isn't just on small businesses, Unit 2 does have links with Unit 1, so don't forget about those topics when you're revising.

On this paper half the marks are for analysis and evaluation.

1) The Unit 2 exam is made up of **multi-part data response** questions.

2) You'll have 1 hour 30 minutes and there are 80 marks available, so again you should be aiming to achieve about a mark a minute.

3) There will usually be two sections, with each section based on a different case study. There will be a range of short-answer and extended questions in each section, so don't spend too long on one section.

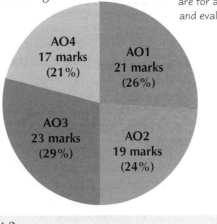

AO4 17 marks (21%)
AO1 21 marks (26%)
AO3 23 marks (29%)
AO2 19 marks (24%)

Calculations to learn for Unit 2

Variance	Unit costs	Labour productivity and Labour turnover
Return on capital	Net profit margins	Capacity utilisation

Get Marks in Your Exam

These pages explain how the exams are marked. Basically, the marks are divided up into four different skills — AO1, AO2, AO3 and AO4, and the more skill levels you hit, the more marks you get. Bit like pinball really...

You get marks for **AO1 (showing knowledge)** and **AO2 (applying knowledge)**

AO1 and AO2 questions usually start with words like "State" or "List".

1) **AO1** marks are for **content** and **knowledge**.
2) This means things like knowing the **proper definitions** for **business terms**.
3) You'll only get about 2 marks for AO1, whether the question is a short one worth 2 marks, a shortish one worth 6 marks or a long one worth 15 marks.

To make sure you'll get marks for content, always give definitions of terms you're using, or formulas if you're doing a calculation.

1) **AO2** marks are for **application** — applying your knowledge to a situation. This means thinking about the **type of business** in the **question**, the product or service it's selling, and the type of market it's in.
2) Numerical **calculations** are also marked as **application**.
3) AO2 is also worth 2-3 marks, but questions which want you to demonstrate AO2 will be expecting you to demonstrate AO1 too, so they'll be worth between 4 and 6 marks overall.

You'll get more marks when you **Analyse (AO3)** and **Evaluate (AO4)**

AO3 marks are for **analysis** — thinking about benefits, drawbacks, causes, effects and limitations.

Analysis questions usually start with words like "Analyse", "Examine" or "Explain why".

1) Use your knowledge to **explain** your answer and give **reasons**.
2) If there's data, say what the figures **mean**, talk about what might have **caused** them and say what **effect** you think they will have on the business in the **future**.
3) For top marks, write about **context** — compare a situation with the industry as a whole, or with a competitor.
4) Consider **both sides** of the **argument** — you can only get **limited** analysis **marks** by looking at **one side**.

AO4 marks are for **evaluation** — using your **judgement**.

Evaluation questions usually start with words like "Evaluate", "Discuss", "Justify" or "To what extent".

1) **Weigh up** both sides of the argument — consider the **advantages** and **disadvantages** and say which **side** of the argument you think is **strongest**.

2) You don't need a **definite** answer. You can point out that it **depends** on various factors — as long as you say **what the factors are**, and say **why** the right choice depends on those factors. Use your judgement to say what the **most important factors** are. The most important thing is to **justify** why you're saying what you're saying.

It floats — but not on the stockmarket.

3) Relate your answer to the **business described in the question** and to the **situation in the question**. Give reasons why **this business** would make a particular decision, and how and why **these particular circumstances** would affect their decision. For example, there's no point saying that Mr Richards might consider floating his business on the stockmarket if he only has a turnover of £280,000 a year — it's just not a realistic choice for a company of that size.

Get Marks in Your Exam

They give marks for How You Write, too

1) You have to use the **right style** of writing and **arrange relevant information clearly** — write a **well-structured essay**, not a list of bullet points. You need to use **specialist vocabulary** when it's appropriate, so it's well worth **learning** some of the **fancy terms** used in this book.

2) You have to write **neatly** enough for the examiner to be able to read it. You also need to use good **spelling**, **grammar** and **punctuation** to make your meaning **crystal clear**. Don't worry, you won't lose marks for spelling errors — but if your handwriting, grammar, spelling and punctuation are **so** far up the spout that the examiner **can't understand** what you've written, **expect problems**.

3) Out of the whole paper, you only get **2** or **3** marks for written communication — but remember that if the examiner can't **read** or **understand** your writing, you won't get the **other marks** either.

Jotting down a quick essay plan will help.

Dudley got no marks for his "Boston Matrix in Mime".

The Examiner will try to show you How Much to Write

1) The examiner does try to help you by telling you how many marks each question is worth and by giving you an idea of how much you need to write.

2) They usually provide about **two lines** for every mark — so for a question worth two marks you'll get four lines.

3) Generally, if the question is worth 2 or 3 marks then you just need to show your business studies knowledge. Give a short answer and move on quite quickly.

4) For a 12 to 15 mark question you need to show analysis and evaluation. You'll have to write much more for these questions. They usually expect you to make a decision, or have an opinion and be able to justify it. There's rarely a right or wrong answer to this sort of question, so just convince the examiner that your opinion is valid by explaining your reasons.

Don't forget to include All the Skills in Extended Answer Questions

1) When you come up against a long question (worth, say, 15 marks), **don't jump** straight to the **evaluation** stage. The examiner will be looking for **evidence** of the **other skills**, too.

2) So, if they ask you how Mr Frimble can increase his profits, and you think he should either increase his mark-up or make some staff redundant, you need to:

> 1) **Define** what is meant by mark-up and redundancy (this will get you your **AO1** marks).
>
> 2) Explain how mark-up/redundancy are **relevant** to the type of **business/ product** that Mr Frimble owns/produces (for **AO2** marks).
>
> 3) Give the **advantages** and **disadvantages** of each method of increasing profits (for **AO3** marks).
>
> 4) Finally, for the **AO4** marks, **weigh up** both sides of the argument and **decide** if Mr Fimble should increase his mark-up or make some staff redundant (you might decide he needs to do both).

For an example of an essay answer which demonstrates all the skills, see p.83.

It's exam time — let's get down to business...

These pages should take some of the surprise out of your exams. You don't need to know this upside down and back to front like you do the actual business studies stuff. What you do need to know is what the examiners actually want to see from you — not just that you know the facts, but also that you understand and can put to use what you've learnt.

Do Well in Your AQA Exam

Here's an example of the kind of case study and questions you may get in Unit 1.

Crinkle Cakes Ltd

Janet Jones had always enjoyed pottering around in her kitchen, and took great pride in the fact that friends and family used to ask her to bake cakes for birthdays and special occasions. However, it was only when one of her friends insisted on paying her £10 for a cake that she first thought of it as a way of making a living.

Eight years on and what had been Janet's sole trader business has grown into a medium-sized private limited company. Although she still plays an important day-to-day role in the business, it is no longer based in her kitchen. The business now operates out of premises equipped with machinery which allows them to produce 50 cakes per hour.

The business operates in a very competitive market which is dominated by two national bakeries. It also faces competition from a long-established local firm, which has an excellent reputation in the area. Janet believes that in order to ensure the long-term survival of the business she needs to look at ways in which Crinkle Cakes Ltd could compete more effectively, and achieve its objective of increasing both sales and market share. Money is tight though, since the premises and machinery were obtained using finance which is still being paid off.

Janet had always hoped to see her cakes on the shelves of the big supermarkets, but so far Crinkle Cakes has been unable to secure a deal to supply any of the major chains. The main reasons the supermarkets gave for not stocking Crinkle Cakes products were that they had a very narrow product range (selling only whole cakes rather than multi-pack slices or individual portions), and that their cakes were priced higher than competing bakeries.

Janet and her marketing director Stephen Simms have spent a considerable amount of time looking at ways to address these issues. Stephen did some market research, and he presented Janet with the results (see Appendix 1).

Meanwhile, Janet spoke to the operations manager in order to discuss costs. Crinkle Cakes had originally aimed at prices no more than 10% higher than supermarket own-brand prices. The reality though is somewhat different (see Appendix 2). Controlling costs is a real headache due to big fluctuations in the price of raw materials, such as flour. This all gave Janet plenty to think about.

Appendix 1
Results from Market Research (Percentage of People Asked)

Product	Purchased weekly	Purchased monthly	Purchased rarely	Never purchased
Family-sized cake	2	8	62	28
Multi-pack, e.g. slices	55	23	14	8
Individual portions	67	17	10	6

Appendix 2
Recommended Retail Price of Competitors' Products

Company	Family cake	Multi-pack	Individual Portions
Crinkle Cakes Ltd	£5.29	-	-
Local Competitor	£5.09	-	£0.59
National Competitor	£4.49	£1.39	£0.55
Market Leader	£4.99	£1.39	£0.60
Supermarket Own Brand	£3.99	£1.19	£0.49

An **Example Question and Answer** to give you some tips:

The business referred to in the article is a private limited company. Outline TWO features of a private limited company. (4 marks)

> A private limited company belongs to its shareholders, who have to be part of the company. The shares cannot be bought by the public and won't be quoted on the stock exchange.
>
> The shareholders of a private limited company have limited liability, which means that they are not personally responsible for the debts of the business. The only money they can lose is the money they have invested in the company.

Both features outlined here are to do with ownership, but there are plenty of other things you can say about private limited companies. Other points that could have been made include the fact that private limited companies don't have a minimum share capital requirement and that they tend to be quite small family-run businesses.

Do Well in Your AQA Exam

An *Example Extended Question and Answer* to give you some tips:

Suggest a marketing strategy that might ensure that Crinkle Cakes Ltd can continue to compete within their competitive market. (15 marks)

Any marketing strategy is based around the idea of the marketing mix. This is more commonly referred to as "the four Ps" of product, price, place and promotion. In order to develop a marketing strategy it is necessary to examine each of these four factors in turn.

A01: Refers to, and defines, marketing mix (2 marks)

There are a number of factors that need to be examined if Crinkle Cakes wish to improve the product aspect of their marketing. At present they appear to produce mainly family cakes, which 28% of customers never buy according to the research findings in Appendix 1.

Make use of information in the case study

In addition this has meant that few supermarkets have shown a willingness to sell Crinkle Cakes' products. As such I would recommend that they sell a wider range of cake sizes. In addition to the full cakes they could introduce a multi-pack containing cake slices, aimed at families, and single-slice packs, perhaps aimed at single people or impulse purchases. This would widen their target market, since they are likely to be purchased by a different type of consumer. One final alteration that Crinkle Cakes could make to their products is to introduce a range of new cake flavours, though this may require further market research.

A04: Makes a sensible recommendation after considering evidence (1 mark)

The price that Crinkle Cakes charge for their products is stated in the case study to be higher than their competitors' prices, yet they also indicate that the target price should be no more than 10% above the own-brand products. If they adopt this strategy then the figures given in Appendix 2 show that Crinkle Cakes' prices would be lower than their main three competitors. The strategy should be continued to pursue the objective of increasing sales and market share. However, the study states that the costs of raw materials have prevented this, so steps to control costs would have to be taken to make this possible. Controlling costs is also important while the business is still paying off the cost of its premises and machinery.

Don't waste time repeating the case study, just refer to it

A02: Links issue of price to business in question (1 mark)

A03: Considers consequences of financial decisions (1 mark)

As far as place is concerned, Crinkle Cakes must take steps to get their products into the major supermarkets. This should be possible if they make the changes to the product size already discussed.

This is a little vague

The case study does not give any detail about what promotion has taken place. Advertising could be a problem, due to the financial constraints of having to raise finance from within. As such, the company may wish to investigate methods of sales promotion involving tie-ups with other companies. This might be particularly useful if new products are to be launched. The company may also wish to use publicity and public relations to raise brand awareness in a more cost-effective way than advertising.

A04: Makes a sensible recommendation after considering evidence (1 mark)

In conclusion, there are a number of recommendations, as outlined, which Crinkle Cakes Ltd should consider in order to make improvements to their marketing mix, and to achieve the objectives that they have set themselves.

Summarising your ideas is a good idea, but make your recommendations clear

Left margin annotations:

Stating knowledge is fine, but don't waste too much time

A02: Links knowledge about marketing mix to business in question (2 marks)

Apply your suggestions to the business in question

It's fine to say you don't think change is needed as long as you explain why

A03: Considers possible risks/ problems (2 marks)

Referring to financial restrictions is always a good idea

A04: Makes vague attempt at overall evaluation (1 mark)

This is a reasonably good answer and would get about **11 marks**. It considers a range of marketing options and applies them to the business in the case study. It also makes excellent use of the **information provided** by the examiner. This answer has been set out sensibly with a separate paragraph for each aspect of the marketing mix.

The conclusion is poor and doesn't add anything to the answer. It would've been better if it had made clear which aspects of the marketing mix should be changed as a priority. Remember that the examiner is looking for **evaluation**, and one way of doing this is to explain why it might be better to take one course of action instead of another.

Index

Index

Index